The Cyberhorny Dream Diaries
Digital journal entries in an ebook by an egirl.

The Cyberhorny Dream Diaries

Digital journal entries in an ebook by an egirl.

Dreamed and Curated by Nastya Valentine
Analyzed by Evan Dunn

Cyberhorny LLC
* Los Angeles   *   Nashville *

Published by:
Cyberhorny LLC
73 White Bridge Rd
Suite 103 #318
Nashville, TN 37205

www.cyber-horny.com

publishing@cyber-horny.com

ISBN: 978-1-962521-01-7

Dedicated to: the players, not the game

If all is but a dream within a dream, then
the little things we worry so much about
are subject to impermanence anyway

DISCLAIMER: This shit kinda ugly but it slaps

Pardon the slipshod design, I am having psychosis
due to just having witnessed spectacular visions....

A foreword before you dive in.......

I have been performing my whole life, on and off camera. To be a woman is to perform. Existence is my art medium. Bedroom is my office. My body is my instrument, my technology. Dreaming (when I'm able to sleep) is my muse.

Every single show/installation/performative art project that I do centers on a bedroom aesthetic being a vital part of the production because I'm always mirroring and integrating, bringing the inner to the outer, the personal space to the performance space, the floor to the ceiling, the unconscious to the conscious, the subjective to the objective, the unknowable to the familiar... or maybe I just want to have an area that's comfortable to bring me peace in case I need a nap or have anxiety...

It would then make sense to see these themes explored in my writing as well, bedrooms and dreams laying out a frontispiece from the ethereal domain.

Cyberhorny Dream Diaries originally came together as a side project from my book Cyberhorny: Navigating A Sexual Dystopia, an academic text about my scope of experiences in the online adult industry. It wasn't supposed to be a full project of its own, rather a cute petite little offshoot to make the full book look good. However, as it developed, and as interest in it grew, not just from others but from myself, this becoming a full piece spoke to me with remarkable clarity. Many of my idols like David Lynch and Carl Jung take strong inspiration from deep dream analysis, yet the practice of it isn't taken seriously or dismissed as frivolous. That's okay. I'm often not taken seriously or dismissed as frivolous. Dream analysis is for the girlies. This book, the art I made for it, the time I spent dissecting my dreams, is my intellectual domain.

My friend and collaborator Evan Dunn lent his expertise in psychoanalysis to interpret my dreams - knowing classical symbolism, and knowing me, he offered incredible insight into the dark, burdenous void of my subjectivity. My business partner Jason Tarkington approached the role of editor when this book fell through with another publisher, and created a situation in which it could be published through our company on a deadline. I would like to thank these men for their professionalism and involvement in this project. See? My whimsical, girly little praxis could indeed be taken seriously sometimes.

Believe it or not, I would also like to thank myself for having the wherwithal and strength to see this to completion. Thank you to my therapist for helping me say this without self deprecation and overcome my cognitive distortions. Without further ado, here goes the Cyberhorny Dream Diaries:

"Extreme seductiveness is at the boundary of horror"
— Georges Bataille

Table of Contents

Good god, get a grip girl.
How do I cope? How do I regulate when I'm dysregulated?
Diaries of a tortured crackhead...

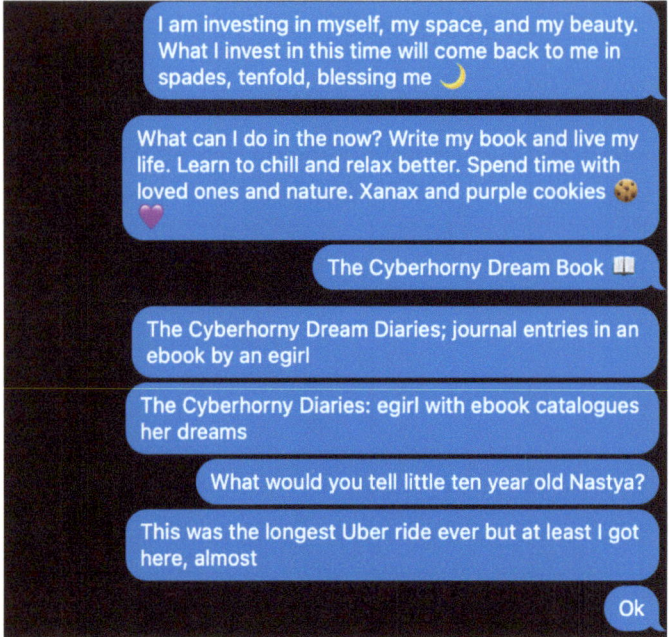

Manic depressive illness be like "if you saw me chilling no you didn't"

How do psychoanalysis, sexuality, and dreams intertwine? It's a question I ask myself with never any clear answers, only more questions interfacing to penetrate my mind. I've done my best to organize my thoughts for this book, but clarity is not my strong suit. I belong to the realm of chaos, coming up for air only when enough is enough. Praxis is not enough.

Ever since I've been able to consciously and intelligently process reality, I have recorded my dreams in an analog notebook diary. I've kept copious collections of notebooks. Dreamlike imagery has always been important in my art, and many concrete ideas start in the vague void of these preconscious flickers. As I fell out of practice with keeping paper journals, the immediacy of frantically tapping out iphone notes replaced the scribble of the pen.

Dreams are remarkable. They can be mysterious, frightening, joyful, violent, deviant, inspiring, prophetic. They can be horny and seductive – we've all had our plethora of sex dreams. They can wake us up asking, "what the fuck was that?" Occasionally, they can be so pleasant that we wish to go back to sleep because the dream is so much more beautiful than the reality.

This is a diary of selected dreams from 2021-2023. Waking up unnerved in the middle of the night, heart racing, or full body sweating, or still drowsy, I took to my iphone notes to record the manifest content in my dreams, as well as random thoughts and feelings that came to mind immediately upon opening my eyes. Anything at all that I can remember. Stream of consciousness ranting. After a few years of documentation, I (along with my psychoanalytic dream interpreter Evan Dunn) have selected a series of significant dreams during this time to dissect.

Dualities are highly present in my waking life so it makes sense that in my dreams they appear as well. In my dreams it's often understood that I'm a highly trained, highly paid, highly skilled assassin or darkweb hitwoman. An assassin, like a camgirl, lives a double life. She hides her alter ego from the players in her first identity, and it could be dangerous or even fatal to reveal who she really is, and what she really does for work. As a camgirl, the parallel is obvious – I too create a separate identity and live strategically, with more fragmentation than integration. My apartment, which of course I know so well, also tends to randomly change layout in my dreams – a duality of what I know to be constant and true, vs what is surreal and unpredictable. There is a recurring dream I have in which I'm back in college and I live in two dorms and I feel unsettled because I failed to graduate or failed to show up for class and now I'm behind.

If "every dream contains a wish" as Freud maintained, then the latent content derived from the manifest content would be as such: assassins are fearless, whereas in the real waking life, my anxiety destroys me. I've put a hit out on myself and I'm going missing. Evan's interpretations of my dreams weave together a narrative for me, and decrypt the symbolism that I may be subconsciously blocked to. Then there is my meta analysis of his analysis - where I react to it in writing - which blends to the point where I almost can't tell the two voices apart. An intersubjective experience. What is that they say about the mind-body problem? The Cartesian dualism vs monism? Reconciling impossible dualities?

Two phones, two hotels, two schools, two dorms.. two lives.

This month, as I write this diary, is around the timeline in which I am waking up in the coma dream. A year and a half after August 2021. Interesting thing about waking up in the middle of the night with an anxiety attack, and working on this. I feel oddly comforted by sleep deprivation and hunger: it reminds me of childhood. My youth was highly punctuated by insomnia, anxiety, and lack of adequate self care. When we go on a journey of self improvement and self actualization, the old self dies to make room for the new. It's cyclical. Real growth is uncomfortable. Rebirth is painful. Birth is our biggest trauma and we spend our whole lives recuperating from it. There is a reason why most of therapy is spent talking about childhood traumas and our often broken relationships with at least one of our parents. To reparent yourself is to set yourself free in this cold, harsh, uncomfortable world, and rip apart the umbilical cord that entwines the danger and the freedom of the high end assassin life-style with the safe, sheltered cocoon of the dreamer's bed.

Ok like my boyfriend is whipped now but.., what if he gets un-whipped?? Nightmares... It's ok to be cracked out and cooched out and slutted up.

Body and soul, brain and hole... two polarities within my self.

These images are reminiscent of Carl Jung's *Red Book*; one of my faves. Evan and I are bringing psychoanalysis back without a gawking ideology. Psycho anal sis. Sus. Y SIS Y. Why? Cause we feel like it. We just like it. We're just like this. Lacanian chitches and Baudrillard's chussy. It's just like a vibe idk. I'm just like really into it rn I'll let u know later. Tetralogy of Fallot. Legend of Zelda. Sleeping in the Teslussy model Y on my lunch break but that's all day cause I don't have a job, actually I work 24/7 and that's f*cked up O_O .. More on that in the main text of Cyberhorny: Navigating a Sexual Dystopia, about how sex work is really shroedinger's job, but anyway I simp-ly don't get enough sleep. 😟 By the time the full book comes out, this will have been an introduction to Nastya Valentine's iconic and legendary Cyberhorny. An appetizer, a pregame, a foreplay, a premonition. Predictive dreams from my coochie chakra.

Sunday 12:54 PM

Where is the couch?

J arising

In the mirror selfie room

Arise and shiiiineee

There's a whole list of shit my parents never did that I now outsource to various emotional containers - subs friends boyfriend therapist

Why I need therapy twice a week fr.. discourse on validation

Girl you need levity!! Play drums !!

Goddamn it I am always just holding myself hostage and throwing away the key

My mom and I are opposites in that she's a ball buster and I boost men's egos for a living

In the moments that I first wake up and regain conciousness, especially after a particularly vivid narrative dream, it's crucial for me to shut off all distractions and pay attention. If I don't, the memory of that dream could be lost forever like a deleted file. Used to be as I'd go about my day, something could trigger that dream memory – but nowadays my attention span, cognition, nervous system, and executive function have gotten so shot that processing for a dream requires a higher level of effort. Deep precision work. In some ways I feel like a short circuiting machine, or a malfunctioning fembot. Who or what will repair me? They say that sleep repairs burnout... if I ever remedy my insomnia it's over for you hoes. God gives his weariest battles to his tiredest sleepyheads. How do psychoanalysis, sexuality, and dreams intertwine? This diary has three main parts. The intro, the dream narratives, (along with Evan Dunn's interpretations of my dreams and AI generated pics), and the endgame. A tertiary drama. Because all of life is a trilogy of the histrionic, and I've always had a flair for punctuating the dramatic. (My psychiatrist calls it OCD).

They fuck you up, your mum and dad. They may not mean to, but they do. They fill you with the faults they had. And add some extra, just for you. ~Philip Larkin

"We live in a world where there is more and more information, and less and less meaning." ~Jean Baudrillard

"Some may never live, but the crazy never die."
— Hunter S. Thompson

"Unhappy parents teach you a lesson that lasts a lifetime."
-J G Ballard

^ Look at my dynamic progress tho: (4)
Guys be committing R, K, M, B, and L big time. -N

I be committing too.. to the psych ward. Miss 5150 over here.

... is it normal he said I have an obese coochie?
I vajazzled my cat and be feeling so skinnylicious ...

I think no matter how I'm dressed it's obvious I'm a slut. I've been told I have the vibe of like: "if a disney princess sent nudes". In the human brain, beauty is pleasure. The urge to be dainty and beautiful because I was always told I was fat and ugly by my own parents. Sluts are beautiful angels, hoes are healers. Sex work is a profession of beauty, the ultimate perversion and distortion of it; the climax of beauty. A facade. The slut becomes the virgin, and back again.. a Carl Jungian enantiodriomia.

Ok but like if as a girl artist you never had a georgia okeeffe vagina pictures/vaguely religious side wound of christ phase have you even lived?

The relationship between a girl and her bedside table. The crucifixion of comfort.

⌒ *Cyberhorny Dream Diaries* ⌒ is as stated previously, somewhat of a work in parallel with my academic piece *Cyberhorny: Navigating a Sexual Dystopia*. It's important to acknowledge the human, the corporeal, the sensorial - juxtaposed with the stimulation overloaded and technologically advanced world we e-exist in. Unlike us degenerate simpletons, AI's can't get horny or have dreams. Can they? Do androids dream of electric titties? We may never know.

The form of this journal is as such:
⌒Dream date and context.

⌒Hastily scrambled iPhone notes, sometimes nonsensical and other times a bit more coherent.

⌒Psychoanalytical interpretation/spiritual discussion/existential takeaway. What are these psychic visions telling me?

⌒Taking from the format of the best show ever, *Criminal Minds*, a quote or two

⌒AI pic: can a program ever render a dream visual, or are these visuals just too ephemeral to be accurately conjured by a non human engineer?

I developed *Cyberhorny* as a project/brand/entity in 2021 and started sharing the initial process of my writing in 2022. Now in 2023 the inner-outer matrix is slowly being broken and what I have bubbled up inside is beginning to bubble on outward. *Cyberhorny* was developed to shatter the stigma that sex workers can't make critiquable art or contribute intellectually to society. That myth is outright false, and in fact almost every SW I know has the characteristics of a healer, educator, artist, therapist, and divine creator. We are chameleonic and absorb parts of other people's psyches. In that, we need to take care of ourselves and nurture our healing.

Energy work is one of the ways we can have a grounding practice in an inherently ungrounded and terminally chaotic line of work. Dreaming and bedtime are a beautiful, sacred practice for me. The bedroom is primarily for sex time and dream time — but it is so much more beyond that, it's a crossroads between astral planes and other dimensions. In dreams, possibilities are limitless and long sought answers can be found. Or even more questions can arise.

Dreams tell us a lot about ourselves. They're complicated and visual. Somehow the visuals are intangible and hard to grasp, distances away, so close and yet so far. In that arena, I have always been curious about how art can portray a dream sequence. Cinema seems to be the most effective medium, but what about a still image - tech has come so far (too far, some may say; perfectly paced, say others) and is so powerful now. Can the current technologies available to consumers create an accurate rendering of our inner unconscious worlds?

Like I would approach a spirit guide in an ayahuasca session, I asked the midi journey AI bot to render my dreams into a picture. These images were the results.

It's 2023, do people still have sex in beds? I actually haven't sexed with a non-work partner since 9/11.... I wish I was kidding. Becoming a virgin again and again. I lose my virginity all the time. Every few years, routinely. For a slut, I'm a huge virgin. The loss of the V card is an outdated concept for a (literally) anti-climactic moment. Don't you think? What was your first time like? Memorable? Unremarkable? Enjoyable? Triggering? Read on to see what Faulker says about female purity, what Sylvia Plath says about marriage, and what Lacan (big L) says about a lot of stuff.

My outfit costs $3500 but being in an abusive relationship with me is free.

cyber-horny.com/shop to buy the Nastya pillow !

Even my Cyberhorny merchandise is within sleep and bedtime aesthetics, as well as a commentary on my own self-objectification.

Discourse of the nastya pillow: it's something you can sleep with and cuddle up for just a short time. This is how men see me. An object. Comfortable, transient, temporary, disposable. Things you used to love will die somewhere in your house or garage. She used to watch you watch your favorite shows as you got comfortable, then her softness and luster faded and now she sits somewhere between an old vacuum cleaner and a pile of obsolete dvds

Men fantasize about sleeping w me

Men sleep on my intellect and talent

Men love sleeping over til they see how many LEDs and plushes I have

🔍   psychoanalysis and **childhood trauma**

🔍   psychoanalysis and **feminism pdf**

🔍   psychoanalysis and **personality**

🔍   psychoanalysis and **dreams**

🔍   psychoanalysis and **trauma**

This is where I post from:

The wave weapon of time is my enemy... Against it,
I'm in combat. Everything is temporary, nothing lasts.

"Be his peace" bitch please I am hand delivering him a
speedball via bomb squad every morning......

Without further ado, attempting to check my ego at the door and releas-
ing the chaos of my dream content, here is the narrative portion of my
dream diaries (bear in mind these are not in a linear order, just in the
order they were written in my phone notes...)

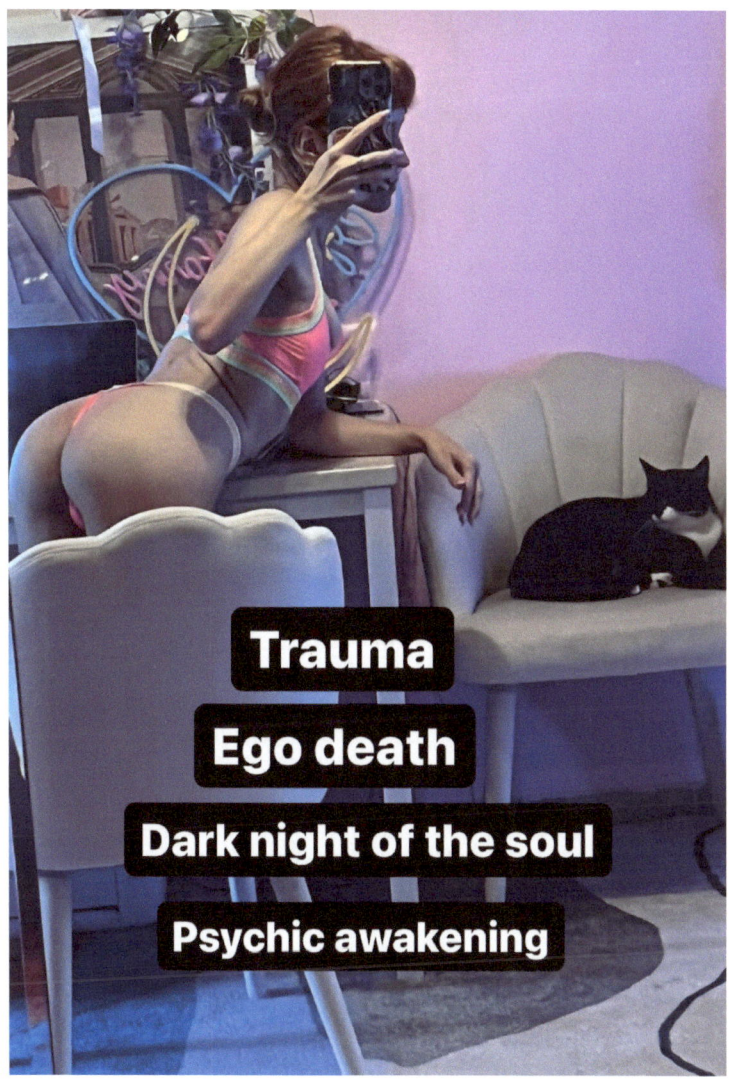

DREAM 1.
UNDATED.
Context: Unknown; 2021

Narrative: House sitting at this house... almost sentient ... let the cat Britney Spears out... outdoors there is a pond with turtles ... Reddit(?) ... one close walls collapsing semblance of family each room had a value
Some people are momentary others are eternal
Become a hollow bamboo so that god can play his music through you
Becoming a work of art, nothing more, abstract tho
I just hope a couple guys wanna stop and stare at my tiny body ▨
Awards rewards in every room, activities in every room 🏠
Be grateful for the good. It will get you through the rest.
You lose someone and every new second is a brand new circle of hell.
People who think and feel in a depth that verges on madness
Fall ass backwards into the looking glass
Not fall into any category; take all ur favorite things and put them in one place
Time prison ✂
A vague dream but I got a lot of epiphanies and downloads

Interpretation:
        House sitting, walls closing in, the figure of britney spears (almost sentient) trapped and let out - a pond with turtles (not frogs although 'reddit'): all images of a thwarted freedom - figures being constrained, an environment artificial and not owned. This motif solidified with the sentence 'some people are momentary other are eternal'. Images of falling allude to the season, a season in which life becomes cold - things fall apart. Nastya is dreaming of losing Don. Some people are momentary. Don did not like activities, he did not like people staring at her tiny body, or the idea that she could do real-life work in the sex industry. He attempted to conserve and constrain her. The terror and madness of the thought of someone being eternal.

Cat named Britney Spears? You better work bitch. Which iteration of Britney was this? Her eras have entered the cultural lexicon and dare I say the collective unconscious as archetypes: teen Baby one more Time Britney, 2007 bald headed Britney hunted by the media, Free Britney in more recent times...

"Something is always born of excess: great art was born of great terror, great loneliness, great inhibitions, instabilities, and it always balances them." — Anaïs Nin

"From the idea that the self is not given to us, I think there is only one practical consequence: we have to create ourselves as a work of art."
— Michel Foucault

DREAM 2.
8 17 22
Context: Day 4 of my reiki practice's psychic reset. I studied under a powerful group of reiki mothers, self-initiated with the unique teachings of Sacred Stripper, who emphasizes the individual finding their own sacred gifts within existing spiritual structures. HOE: Heaven on Earth reiki is a powerful medicine, the focused practice of which manifests great changes into life.

Narrative:
I was in a one and a half year coma. I worried: who had access to my notebooks?
Got up immediately upon waking - A reset of the resets
Two phones - contacted Evan; friends in group chat up to same shiz
Mom didn't leave my side
Still in a high OF % % after long absence

Where is. Bae? What evidence did I leave behind the life of struggling/repairing?
I did not want him access to my life's work.
Saw some seals playing with icicles

Interpretation: Wouldn't it be nice to be in a coma. The only problem is that life keeps going and when you wake up it is still there.

"Death belongs to the realm of faith. You're right to believe that you will die. It sustains you. If you didn't believe it, could you bear the life you have? — Jacques Lacan

"The most important thing you do in your life is to die."
— Timothy Leary

Two phones, two nastyas - one present one gone. If I remain in a coma I am not dating. I am in a comma - a split between the prior subject and the next. I remain hidden and unaccessed by him. The notebooks must remain unopened. Two quotes. Bookended and frontispieced. Epilogue and prologue. End and beginning. After and before. Disorder and clarity. I want to be in control of my life - out of his control but sometimes the easiest way to control it is to leave it.

DREAM 3.
8/21/21
Context: what's happening in waking life? The OF porn ban in full force, I am concerned for my job and my livelihood. Considering irl sex work but because I have a bf who dislikes the idea of me doing it, I stay online.

Dystopian Elon's handmaids dream:
Basically his own city/baby factory
A demented Tesla castle and male hierarchy
The choice of women was doing through song - It was a "play" "performance"
The women he chose based on an algorithm but me and one woman discovered the secret

We tried to save animals and children and women
Grimes was brainwashed into Elon's evil at first but then became scared and wanted to expose; he killed her
He was king of the city-state and had priests
He imprégnanted us after making us pass out, bred the most submissive weak and attractive women then enhanced the uterine dna
To the woman who figured it out, they murdered her in a garage of cars
I hacked one Tesla to submit to me and survived

The priest sent me an animal in a blender as a symbol of what he would do to me; I honored the animal, drank its blood, cried and broke mirrors
I murdered the priest slowly doing basically what he did to the animal, after seducing him under the guise that I was innocent/into it
I got revenge and then gave myself an abortion
As for Elon I had a plan and rigged his personal devices; since he didn't pay attention to women and underestimated us, we were to be his downfall

Interpretation: Being a woman is difficult. Being a woman with a dad can be even worse.
(Theoretically) if the laws set forth by the father are not integrated into the subjectivity of the child this is when psychosis is activated. Nastya struggles to see her father as an authority (perhaps as he has not proven to be one) and what ensues is indeed psychotic: animals in blenders, abortions, murders, blood drinking, etc. The anger of her waking life towards him has disseminated itself into her work, her relationships with cold and distant men, and her closeness with the mother. The dream presents a much simpler solution. The psychosis is repeated - in other words Nastya inherits the violent apathy of the father and inverts it as a solution to the genesis of the problem itself.

'The father, the Name-of-the-father, sustains the structure of desire with the structure of the law -- but the inheritance of the father is that which Kierkegaard designates for us, namely, his sin.' - Jacques Lacan

"My blood alone remains. Take it. But do not make me suffer long." ~Marie Anotinette

DREAM 4.

12 12 22

Context: A month after my birthday and a month after ayahuasca trip; initial stages of reintegration are happening. I watched a lot of Rupauls Drag Race during this time. I received some holiday presents from my clients. It felt really nice to be thought about, and to be (literally) gifted.

In front of rupaul (kind of a horror dream)

Back to the esthetician salon.. Adore Delano was working there named as Orochi or something

Hotel, two of them: not two schools anymore

One room was all private for me burgundy and gray decoration

Second room was bigger and more luxurious but bisected (?) by guests

Mother had found and saved my nudes and OF profile so I took her phone to delete them

Amazon and deliveries were coming ...

Interpretation: Drag itself is quite dream-like. Subjects with two meanings. Men with both genders, two hotels. The desire that escapes from this narrative is for the mom to find out what the daughter is doing. Horrifying on the conscious level - unconsciously the wish is to bridge the gap - for Nastya to stop doing drag as a good daughter and be real with the mom. The deliveries and amazon are unstoppable. A rapprochement between mom/daughter is forced by the gifts of the OF simps. It is the gift.

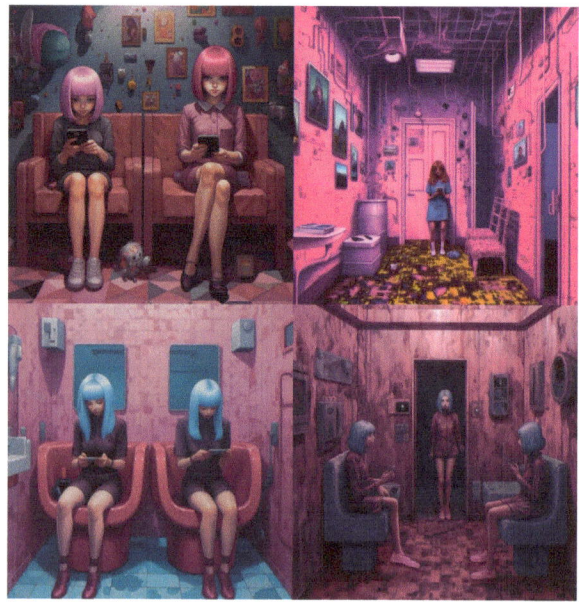

3c: Rapprochement theory (Margaret Mahler): (14-24 months) At this point the child's desire to achieve independence is marred by a fear of abandonment. Therefore, the child seeks to maintain proximity to the caretaker while engaging in exploration.

"Don't piss on my leg and tell me it's raining" ~Bianca Del Rio, as Judge Judy on RPDR

"The Universal Mother is also the death of everything that dies. The whole round of existence is accomplished within her sway, from birth, through adolescence, maturity, and senescence, to the grave. She is the womb and the tomb." ~Joseph Campbell

DREAM 5.
1 1 2023
Context: it's the new year bitchhhhhh time 2 fuckin party I feel a change in the air; it was raining like crazy like harder than I may have ever seen in LA ; went to Celeste's house for a casual NYE we been doing that for the past few years like lowkey but party, thank god no hangovers since I stopped drinking (only a lil bit sometimes 🎉 ☺)

At a hotel or my apartment altered
Wanted to visit my mom
None of my devices working properly
Would only send mixed pictures: maps, screenshots, uncontrollable pics..
Mom either didn't see or blocked her sight or accepted me cause she texted me back "your video sold" "you look like Sean young"
There were planes flying in the courtyard and angry loud neighbors
I tried to get an Uber and get my cat into her bag
Meanwhile irl my mom and Victor having a text argument and I was in the group chat witness..

Interpretation: another variation on a theme dream/nightmare in which the mother finds the pictures - purportedly on accident. Nastya has posed as bladerunner girl on OF. Trying to get the cat into her bag. Trying to get mom to understand the pussy makes the money. It is hard to become human with our parents. " 'More Human Than Human' Is Our Motto." -Rachael, Blade Runner.

The pictures are always uncontrollable. But it is simultaneously the only way to control what people think about you. To try to use pictures. At least it is easy than text. You can have arguments with text. I'm always arguing with text. A picture is incontrovertible

"No matter how much you think you love somebody, you'll step back when the pool of their blood edges up too close."~ Chuck Palahniuk

"Even the technology that promises to unite us divides us" ~ Dan Brown

DREAM 6.
3 20 23 Context: A time of beginning work on Cyberhorny book. A new journey.

Seth macfarlane
Working on a production design job that turned into a Castle - ice sculpture snow sculpture all these weird little sculptural ideas
Bumper stickers of my merch: socialist shit
I am a socialist i like sitting on the couch and my favorite thing is pussy 🐱
Something like that
I showed him my work and he's like wow I'm so hard rn and we had sex I think
Then I continued working on the project improving it every time and he came on to me again but I didn't mind I liked it

Interpretation: it's hard to find people you like to have sex with. Especially if your job is pretending. A wish is present here for connection between those online who like her for her ideas (but who may do nothing for her in *that* sense) and the physical in-person dimension of real sexuality.
'We had sex i *think'* is not a question but an assertion. Thinking about sex can be enough.

We had   sex i think
Is different than   we had sex, i think?
Sex i think
Sex i think
All Nastya does is think about sex.
I didn't *mind* I liked it -   sometimes the mind isn't
enough for sex

"Women are never virgins. Purity is a negative state and therefore contrary to nature." – William Faulkner

"We are never so defenseless against suffering as when we love." ~Dr Sigmund Freud

DREAM 7.

4 28 23

Context: Haven't been writing in diary, doing reiki, any sort of self care for a while. This is the winter of my life. A dark night of the soul. Finally I have some time to read, and to write, a rare luxury. My impostor syndrome tells me I don't deserve it.

Weird sleep paralysis and heart rate throughout, in and out of the dream
Cave apartments and neon signs everywhere
Hot guy unsubs
Gaslighting drug to hallucinate reality not being as is
Making it hard to trust myself
Wow that was a scary one
Had to turn the tv on to get out of this dream cause it keeps wanting to pull me back in
The dream was violating me
The anatomy of a kiss from beginning to end and into another
Isn't it fucked up how our consciousness works sometimes

I got R'd by a hot stranger..
Living in Houses made of rock and cave apartments ; neon signs
Internet people living in caves, flipping tarot cards - the devil
My apartment was 107 an elite one but on the 8th floor
I work as stripper :' Riley
Reviews of Cyberhorny
Negative ones were from subs who were simping.. lol the duality

Interpretation: it is not as simple as finding symbolism in the dream to make sense of the waking life. Often the symbolism of the waking life must be used to make sense of the dream. Dreams are less interpretive to real life than they are parabolic. One cannot scry the dream alone for a prophecy or a hidden meaning it must reverberate. If the wish is to be violated the effect will impress itself upon the dreamer using whatever nouns it wants.

Hot guy unsubs can be read in the criminal minds parlance* of unsubstantiated. Is there any of Nastya's own desire at play in the OF. Some effect is had on her libido. She is being violated by her dream.

*Unsub = Unknown Subject

The number 8 in some analyses of the tarot represents cycles (infinity signs when turned 90degrees) - the cards of 8 are the Devil and the World. One's ability to transcend and go beyond the material.

"The need to go astray, to be destroyed, is an extremely private, distant, passionate, turbulent truth."
— Georges Bataille

"Kiss me, and you will see how important I am."
— Sylvia Plath, The Unabridged Journals

DREAM 8.

8 15 22

Context: Don and I started having relationship problems. It seems he could not save me or protect me, the goddess had to do it.

In a dilapidated house, part of a little 'almost' town that's like a project for some entity perhaps or a large school. I'm watching MzNeon's video w Don, Celeste and Mario, and other couples. I had received some gifts from my mom like a new nice bikini.

It was late when we departed, they went a little earlier than us. I couldn't rescue a kitten, it was smaller than a fingertip, and three more were feral and seemed to fend well for themself. We were leaving slowly in the groups. There was some game going on.

It was night, moon was visible and feelable. Different parts of the place had different games. Even in the film there was some, although we didn't particularly participate. MJ and David did. Then we went by an abandoned house and a "pugs/dogs" symbol was visible and knowable.

Suddenly a song started playing "%~%~%~~~objects unknown" and massive amounts of dogs on hybrid dog-wagon chariots stampeding the street/freeway like demon dogs - I am sure they killed some people. "Objects unknown" was part of the game; we went into the abandoned house and did our best to hide because it was not just the dogs, there were entities that the dogs heralded and the entities yelled "objects unknown!!!" and got ready to kill; - looks like if anyone was holding onto an object - unknown to whom it is unclear - they were prob gonna kill everyone anyway — they would be killed. The entities were dark and loud. They created and fed off of fear. Deus ex machina: the butterfly goddess descended in lights and saved us.

Interpretation:

The cat that can't be rescued, the kittens that fend well for themselves i:e on their own. The dream is pointing nastya back into the wilderness away from her relationship. Easy to escape if you're smaller than a fingertip and if there's games going on. You may need to escape if there's games going on. Cats/pussy/feminine sexuality cannot be housed in the same way that men are put into the dog house.

A discrepancy between the uncontrolled feral cats and the controlled (yet by whom) killer dogs.

The image nastya portrays to the world on OF is an object. Her self is unknown.

We all love to be objectified but it can be easier to tolerate (less embarrassing) if those doing it are unknown.

Is the world a dog house where unrestrained men's desires are mediated onto the OF sphere? Is the saving grace going to have to be a deus-ex-machina - a butterfly goddess? Anima vs animus? Animals.

"Men are not gentle creatures who want to be loved, and who at the most can defend themselves if they are attacked; they are, on the contrary, creatures among whose instinctual endowments is to be reckoned a powerful share of aggressiveness.
As a result, their neighbor is for them not only a potential helper or sexual object, but also someone who tempts them to satisfy their aggressiveness on him, to exploit his capacity for work without compensation, to use him sexually without his consent, to seize his possessions, to humiliate him, to cause him pain, to torture and to kill him. Homo homini lupus [man is wolf to man].
Who, in the face of all his experience of life and of history, will have the courage to dispute this assertion?" — Sigmund Freud, Civilization and Its Discontents

"Zugzwang." ~the alias of Adam Worth, Criminal Minds
(A term in chess when the player realizes they'll inevitably be checkmated, the opposite of a deus ex machina.)

DREAM9.

9 13 22

Context: unbeknownst to me, this was the last time I would have sex until ????????????? TBA

Elon liked to rip his missteresses teeth out
I was looking for a house/escrow
With my mom and friends in a major common work area I run into him, he's kind of nice and funny at first
We exchange computer stuff and info
When we were alone he did it casually while smiling and I was in excruciating pain
Have some friends helping me get revenge
He did it to grimes too and then she got brainwashed and started doing it herself... "this one took me two hours" demonic bride
She ripped her own teeth out too, Elon sperm has a meta ability that causes brainwashing
I tortured him in the end, still adjusting my tooth, walking away knowing I took him and his company down and can continue to move on in my new house w my new money .. to rid the world of Elon's sperm while also profiting from that very particular agenda

Interpretation: Does the misspelling of mistresses point to something within the dreamscape? It is the first miss that jumps out to us, however 'mister-esses' alludes to a homosexuality or perhaps in the case a lack of identification with manliness needed in the father or in the partner to make the dreamer satisfied. What do we need teeth for. To speak? To eat? Grime grimes grimace grimaces
Elon, the symbolic father, and violence come together again in the psychotic blender of the unconscious. If the dream really is a letter, to whom is Nastya addressing it?

If sperm has a meta ability that causes brainwashing then you never have to resent your mom from loving your dad more than you. From being more than mom. The oedipal/elektra complex is resolved.

Men can break your heart but that doesn't mean you're a lesbian.

"So I began to think maybe it was true that when you were married and had children it was like being brainwashed, and afterward you went about as numb as a slave in a totalitarian state." -Sylvia Plath

"So generation after generation of men in love with pain and passivity serve out their time in the Zone, silent, redolent of faded sperm, terrified of dying, desperately addicted to the comforts others sell them, however useless, ugly or shallow, willing to have life defined for them by men whose only talent is for death."
— Thomas Pynchon, Gravity's Rainbow

DREAM 10.

10 04 22

Context: This was after I came back from NY film festival that screened a movie made about my OF, and before I went to Italy. On a break with bf, at crossroads of break up or not. To B or not to B. I still loved him, but I could not foresee a future. Quite torn, torn indeed. Can't dissociate from feelings

Crazy dream about Honey Birdette store theft, meth break up, Don and I were breaking up I knew he was doing meth and lying about it ; I was stressed about phone storage space, living in camgirl mansion type house in ABQ or something, packin up my car to leave New Mexico Gucci store: phone, space, combative convo, all mixed up.. Highly trained assassin mixed up in feelings of love. Was I a pimp? He interrupted my arrest.. Did I want to go to jail to get away from him? Cuz if you go to jail you're not actually in jail.

Interpretation riff: doing meth is a great reason to break up with someone. An assassin has power, of course, and we might say Nastya felt powerless in the relationship - but what is really at play here is the desire to be able to kill one's feelings.

"The rifle is the first weapon you learn how to use, because it lets you keep your distance from the client. The closer you get to being a pro, the closer you can get to the client. The knife, for example, is the last thing you learn." -Leon, 'Leon: The Professional' (assassin movie).

"You can't be a pimp and a prostitute too" ~Jack White, Icky Thump

DREAM11.

10 17 22

context: (and context on boy 0?) NOPE !!!!!! sorry 😂 is he Italian? I'll never tell..

the dream I had about boy 0 in Italy: we were set up by a mutual friend, in Italy.. We both traveled from far away to this place just to meet each other, away from our significant others; he actually saw me before the arrangement, I was running and shimmering like a unicorn in slow motion wearing all pink, with pink hair, everything ethereal about this moment like a girly Wes Anderson film. Then we met up and recognized each other right away, he was dressed like a gentleman, we went back to his hotel, and then I can't fully remember what happened afterwards.. I think it might have been disappointing, dream-reality not living up to dream-fantasy/expectation; once the tension and longing was gone, there was nothing real underneath that

Interpretation:Is there some part of Nastya that did desire Don? The manifest lesson I suppose is 'don't cheat'. A super-egoic moral impera- tive. But dreams do not belong to the super-ego. This is the most violent of the dreams. The most crushing and psychotic. The fantasy of escaping the relationship is just as disappointing as staying in it. No sex. No love. Nothing real. The wish here is to be left alone

The Palace of Phallus. The Chussy Palace. Floor plans ?? Floor time !!
^ Long hallway ending in two rooms // womblike, pink, and cervical ^

Love set you going like a fat gold watch.

"When one loves, it has nothing to do with sex... Desire, a function cen- tral to all human experience, is the desire for nothing nameable. *((*boy 0 is missing a name.. absolute zero*))* And at the same time this desire lies at the origin of every variety of animation. If being were only what it is, there wouldn't even be room to talk about it. Being comes into existence as an exact function of this lack." -Jacques Lacan

"I'll lock my heart away deeper ..
if I do that ..
I won't have to feel pain outside or inside .. or the fear
I won't have to feel anything at all !" ~from Neon Genesis Evangelion

I'm putting a hit out on myself and going missing

DREAM12.

10 25 22

Context: After coming back from Italy, and before my birthday.

Unholy meridian: Doomed performance at the Hydroelectric dam
Earthquake at the hydroelectric dam; first a small one, then another
small one that turned big; they tried to set the dam to spin in a direction
that remedied the earthquake but it didn't work

I used a little cloth as a reverse parachute to somehow defy physics and
catch wind and it wound up propelling me to a safer place with a few
other survivors

It one of the last days I was abroad, performing at this performing arts
space with lots of creative people; an interesting foreign policy where
once the time started people could not come in and had to wait outside;
some ppl took smoke breaks, I saw "my gays". I had a solo performance
but also with a guy who was Peteresque (my ex) - it was an impassioned
performance. It was sexual, violent, messy, dark, entangled, poetic, aesthetic, creative, chaotic.

I also helped with the aesthetics of a performance prior, and a light blew
up and I think killed the performer. There were a lot of casualties in this
dream

My own little parachute: how did I figure that out? I don't know. I just
knew. It was a natural disaster and I survived by the skin of my teeth or
whatever

Interpretation:

the dam breaks. This kind of symbolism is not uncommon. In the Jungian persuasion water represents the unconscious. Easy enough. The
damn breaks and finally a creative breakthrough. Parachuted into a
scene. Skin of the teeth reclaimed from Elon. Just maybe a casual death
not a murder. Psychosis is sidelined when creativity is embraced.

A natural disaster not as in earth bound calamity but something that was
about due to happen.

People could not come in and had to wait.

Do not come. What is she waiting for? Smoke breaks after the dam
breaks.

'My own little parachute: how did I figure that out?' is a sad thought to
have. Referencing a catastrophic need to escape.

I also analyzed this personally as the relationship being a natural disaster
that I couldn't save even with the dam's advanced technology; using the
tools made it even worse; when it comes down to it, rip off the band aid
rather than letting the wound fester. This will let it heal. Girls like to be
desired. Our boner is validation. Was I getting enough?

"Civilised life, you know, is based on a huge number of illusions in which we all collaborate willingly. The trouble is we forget after a while that they are illusions and we are deeply shocked when reality is torn down around us." ~ J.G. Ballard

"What I wouldn't give for a hot girl. Hell, after all this time, I'd even take an ugly one, if she came with a paper bag."
    ~astronaut Tom Richwood

DREAM13.

11 07 22

Context: before my birthday and ayahuasca trip, beginning dieta and cleanse and meditations

Evan and some of my friends on a rollercoaster in this crazy theme park, certain hz 888 666 222 etc jawline feet meow meow shapes
The Chair next to the door - small beige chair
Fairy coming through the fog - very twin peaks
A twin peaks / return-esque experience
Apocalyptic feeling - the end of the end of the world
A Castle / fortified area like Vatican that was huge and like a mystical city on its own
Walking thhhrroooouuugghhh this fog
General magickal surrealness
Walking a big girl to "retire" her last shows
Climbing a tree only to find a boy and a girl
The girl said "you should have seen this rave!"
Walking in the castle walls
Each room/wing was for a different purpose
Beautiful courtyard
There was some king decreeing
But still an entity/entities guiding
Innocent boy walking with girl
Taken by the devil into the evil castle
He did nothing wrong but paid for his mothers sins
Tarot boards devil coming through them
Hiérophante
You can do everything right, but if ur parents fuck up, ur fucked

Interpretation:
"'The Hierophant is the masculine counterpart to The High Priestess. He is also known as the Pope or the Teacher in other Tarot decks and is ruled by Taurus.' "
Ah Taurus. the lamest zodiac sign, obsessed with comfort and pathetically docile, like a eunuch happy to be jailed if the cell has a bed.
"The Hierophant is a religious figure sitting between two pillars of a sacred temple – though this temple differs from the one in which the High Priestess sits."

Guided by the image of the male high priest, the castle, temple, everything is oh so magical. Fog, the devil, a dark castle, a whole hero's journey. But that would be the easy route of thinking. Everything has a subjective analysis, objectivity is a fallacy – it does not exist.

Paying for the mother's sins - Nastya is often ensconced and misses parts of her own life that must be lived. 'You should have seen this rave.' Even that is muted. 'Seen it' yes, you should have *been at* this rave? A different question. Friends are on the roller coaster while she is going through a fog trapped between castles - trapped in fantasy.

I was actually on the roller coaster in that dream too, but I can see how without syntax and more accompanying writing (the swift, maniacal jotting down of dream moments doesn't really allow for much editing and introspection) it could be misinterpreted, down to just simply what the words are. I stay in a lot and get derided for doing so, but it's the way I live my life. Maybe I need a partner who will take me out to fun and interesting places with an assertive attitude, and spontaneous high budget adventures abroad. I better renew my passport for 2024. I require that type of stimulation from a partner, so yeah like while I am a homebody I also crave adventure but I have to feel safe and secure and not have my boundaries pushed. With a sense of unsafety in my life, I naturally prefer to stay in. Truth be told I don't care if my friends party without me, I know I'll catch up with them later in a more extroverted phase of life. Right now, tho, this is the way it is. It just is. There's a lot going on behind closed doors that people don't know about, can't empathize with, don't understand, or don't want to understand. That's okay tho, the pendulum will swing back one day. I have experienced many a Jungian enantiodromia re: introversion/extroversion and my trauma-influenced activities. My past contains too much hard partying so the scales have to even out. I don't feel that I miss parts of my life that must be lived, if I am in a gilded cage it is of my own making and volition. I have the opposite of Fomo. What am I missing out on when I have everything I need and I don't want to take unnecessary risks? I do a lot already, in fact I'm hyperproductive and I do what I can. Some of the stuff I don't really feel comfortable talking about outside like therapy and stuff, but fuck.. This is a start.

The devil fucks us all eventually, you can't just retire the big girl. The umbilical chord is going to be cut. Out of the castle of the womb and into the devil's realm we must all go.

"When you drop the idea of predicting the future, you start to experience the cards as a mirror of the psyche. That`s when playing with the tarot becomes a path to wisdom."
— Philippe St Genoux

Like the sea that
tumbles on the sand
here the lovers act
as seems good to them
And nobody asks
if it's for the night or
just a while
nobody talks of the
price of this room
of live green velvet
Hyde and Jeckyll Park
public Eden where one hears
night and day
whispered
"the Devil save the Dream!"- jacques prevert

"Hell is empty and all the devils are here."
— William Shakespeare, <u>The Tempest</u>

DREAM14.
3 1 22
Context: don't remember, springtime was a blur, but I was raising my
Little Cat and got her spayed
With dad in Beverly Hills getting drunk
Blackout
Before I know it it's not 11pm it's 3am

Interpretation:
11pm-3am. What happened to Nastya when she was 4 years old.
Is the drive to connect with dad or disconnect from life, or is it both. Getting drunk is an easy way to pass the time

"Who has never killed an hour? Not casually or without thought, but carefully: a premeditated murder of minutes. The violence comes from a combination of giving up, not caring, and a resignation that getting past it is all you can hope to accomplish. So you kill the hour." You do not work, you do not read, you do not daydream. If you sleep it is not because you need to sleep. And when at last it is over, there is no evidence: no weapon, no blood, and no body. "
- mark danielewski

"My father deeply loved both of his parents, but he also despised all that goodness, the white picket fence and all that. He has a romantic idea of that stuff, but he also hated it because he wanted to smoke cigarettes and live the art life, and they went to church and everything was perfect and quiet and good. It made him a little nutty."
~Jennifer Lynch, daughter of David Lynch

DREAM 15
8 1 22
Context: Cyberhorny as a project was slowly starting, and I just hosted Cyber Castle, an art show

Drug dealing and looking at counterfeit pills
Round white ones, slightly off divider line
Classroom, children, YouTube aspirations, nutsack kid w bad behavior and big money - Lola commented on his sincere blog then he deleted it. Ballsack kid put a picture of a pussy instead of a face on his nut sack, paraded it on holidays, his parents were embarrassed, he was matter of fact and opened a portal with his balls — it kinda showed another world, a suburban one
Throwing nuts against a tree and contemplating about genetic studies and longevity studies, study what is important to you in life whether it's school or self study
Got Brandon out of class, big gay dragon as a distraction, saw kitties in a freezer box, and a dog, saved them from the cold
Outside the classroom there were cool college girls, colorful clothes and stuff, my crew felt shy talking to them, I was just "there", one of the girls was really nice "omg hi gang" and we went to her place to get ready. They were doing cool stuff like video shoots and styling and enjoying themselves
I dressed up, Pamela Anderson vibe in red vinyl pleather clothes and high heels 👠, short tight skirts big blonde hair. Feeling an expiration date on

my existence like I was bout to disappear. I saw Don and we had sex on a beautiful white framed bed in pink hotel which then turned into my bed at home. My man cum in a big heart shape on my body. I still had money hidden under my bed

New Years - I woke up at the ball drop. Was alone in a dark neighborhood. Called miranda to pick me up. Gathered my stuff and started walking. Chose not to help strange men load their truck. Walked swiftly to wal mart, I was armed. I'm safe. She picked me up.

Bass house - $395/mo. To rent from animal collective. I inquired "I'm an older woman, semi retired, who wants to enjoy life"

We are not guaranteed a tomorrow

I have faced a thousand tomorrows but they have all been guiding me to this one.

Interpretation:

Cum on my body money under the bed. Weapons begin gaining prominence. A uniquely perverse dream but in a sense very sterile. Animal collection. Don't ask me how many pokemon are in my apartment. Do not open the freezer. nut on the tree load in the truck cum on the body Pamela anderson vibe: a sex symbol but not a porn star

are the drugs real are the drugs fake.

Something here is happening with the partial objects cum, balls, loads, - some are correct and belong with the body - that of her mans. But loads of strange men are to be swiftly dodged.

Throwing nuts against a tree - study genetic longevity. Could there be another reading: did i really come from this sperm. Study the genetics am I my father's daughter. Am I my mother's sins?

'Study what is important to you' - cut to brandon a friend who is constantly studying something that may not be so important to him.

I have faced a thousand tomorrows but they have all been guiding me to this one.

A pleasant shift. A dream like a tomorrow, can positively orient you towards the future. Nastya is feeling hopeful for once?

I think I was feeling hopeful.. There is only so much depression one can take before trying a little bit of optimism. Few things in the world make me feel truly happy, I often feel like the very concept and embodiment of joy has been robbed from me, I have been R'd of my ability to feel joy, peace, and safety, and this type of shit takes years to unlearn. The body keeps score. Trauma is stored in the balls.

"Sex is now a conceptual act, it's probably only in terms of the perversions that we can make contact with each other at all."
— J.G. Ballard

"Everything in the world is about sex except sex. Sex is about power."
— Oscar Wilde

"You know a real friend?
Someone you know will look after your cat after you are gone."
— William S. Burroughs, Last Words: The Final Journals

DREAM16.
8 8 22 - 8 10 22
Context: Watching Pamela series on Hulu.
Hell of a dream sequence
On the moon (trilogy?)
As part of a space force of bard college or something
Several classes were in it
Joining forces with a force containing tommy lee
I had two psychic awakenings
Tommy Lee was set on using this forces resources to destroy the moon, he was like some evil deity
I had to seduce him to save the world
My first psychic awakening was a realization; pretty much when I first started on the mission, what I had to do intuitively
My second psychic awakening was at the most dire time, I was in the bathroom of a geodesic tower trapped with a coworker. Tommy Lee was gonna kill us, I headed outside to escape and survive, no more glasses or weapons left, I thought it was all over. Suddenly I look to my right and am overcome with clarity, I see clear and even beyond. I am the weapon, I Weaponize myself to find Tommy Lee and subconsciously know exactly what to do to destroy his plans

Interpretation:
Obviously worth noting tommy lee is present in a negation, a negative or even a cancelation of positive pamela from the prior dream. Mom good dad bad. I am the weapon. (Nastya has begun to mirror the evil power of the mind-control sperm and etc violent paraphernalia of overlord elon in prior dreams.) The assassin has been found within. As agency returns to Nastya she begins to positively internalize power. Humans only want 4 things and its disgusting. Fuck sleep eat kill. Homo lupus . wolf of the world. Seduction into destruction.
Annilihate the simp commander. The simps are easy prey, tommy lee is an evil mastermind.
Nastya needs a partner who can challenge her not a simp. Don was a simp in the beginning. The conflict is: that in fact it is far more dangerous to be the weapon - being the weapon is being vulnerable and honest with a partner. Onlyfans is a money maker but also a way to master desire, to overcome rejection, to control the space of desire.

*When Don stopped simping, I stopped loving him.

This is not as heartless as it sounds: in the beginning he wooed me with gifts, loving words, promises of being my prince and always taking care of me and balling out for me. This was not a sustainable thing and for various reasons we could not meet each other's needs. I did not want to relinquish sex work because this is how I make my living and he did not like that. He said I have "other options" and he would rather I be "a career woman and not unstable" I'm like if you wanted a stable bitch go ride a horse. No other option is going to be the combo of lucrative + enjoyable for me. Ladies' choice. "Normal" work is miserable and unsustainable for me... kms. I loved that he was a sensitive man but he also referred to himself as a fragile flower when I compared myself to one, saying that I need a man to take care of me and I'm tired of steering. He was worried that I was gonna leave him but the truth is I am incredibly loyal when with a partner who I love. Sex work is my job at this time and unless a man can pay my bills and keep me safe, then my job is more important. It's true that I need a partner who can both challenge me and worship me. It's a delicate balance, a multistep dance, an impossible thought experiment. Perhaps boy 0 doesn't even exist which is why 0 is not even a real number. Who would actually want to date, love, marry a demanding, chaotic, incredulous mess like me?

But as we know from big L:
"In the intervals of the discourse of the Other,
there emerges in the experience of the child something that is radically mappable, namely, He is saying this to me, but what does he want?
In this interval intersecting the signifiers...is the locus of what...I have called metonymy. It is there that what we call desire crawls, slips, escapes, like the ferret."

"The most terrifying fact about the universe is not that it is hostile but that it is indifferent, but if we can come to terms with this indifference, then our existence as a species can have genuine meaning. However vast the darkness, we must supply our own light." ~ Stanley Kubrick

DREAM17.

8 1 21

Context: before OF porn ban.

Instagram monetizing posts ; a prophetic dream?

Go back after a break and see 🔲 €63.96

An angel of the devil himself an influencer hugged me close and said it's okay

I was in school living in dorms "I haven't been in my dorm or home to classes or done my homework in a.... While" sudden realization then that what if I won't graduate

Then the angel said to me this .. "it's a secret"

I packed up all my shit with help from college advisor guy, did some apocalyptic decluttering, hair in a jar I ditched in a cul de sac

Gave a small speech about the importance of paying small artists

Some kind of evacuation / escape

Interpretation:

A profit-ec dream. Instagram has been an angel and a devil it gives and it takes away.

Hair in a jar. Nastya slowly morphs into a christ like figure in the passing of time in her unconscious. Devils and Angels constantly going back and forth. Angel of the devil. Not forming arguments but forming a mobius strip. Crucified by simps. Her own desire thwarted. Sinful yet immaculate. A young college girl still in the dorms yet a 30 year old woman. Madonna/whore blah blah blah. Scalping divinity out of a profane mindset. The traditional idea behind these dreams of missing course-work and delayed graduations is that something in the past remains yet unresolved. Some proverbial assignment is bleating out to be completed. Its a secret

Just put the hair in the jar. Put the body into the world and let the soul fly. Get rid of it. A small speech a small artist a small and profane escape from the cul de sac the college the instagram. The sins of the mother and the father weighing heavy. The sins of the simps also weigh upon her. A dm inbox full of 'can you unblock me' 'can you send me a pic'. Human connection is only a cipher for perversion in the end. A small speech in the dms begging for 63.96 of pussy.

"Stars in my hair in my hair and beard i am crowned with stars christ by his own hand an auto-gethsemane carved darkly out of pure space but not rigid no .. an unmuscled wallowing fecund and foul the placid tragic body of a woman who conceives without pleasure bears without pain." - Faulkner

«No more Internet. No more social media, no more scrolling through litanies of dreams and nervous hopes and photographs of lunches, cries for help and expressions of contentment and relationship-status updates with heart icons whole or broken, plans to meet up later, pleas, complaints, desires, pictures of babies dressed as bears or peppers for Halloween. No more reading and commenting on the lives of others, and in so doing, feeling slightly less alone in the room. No more avatars.»
— Emily St. John Mandel

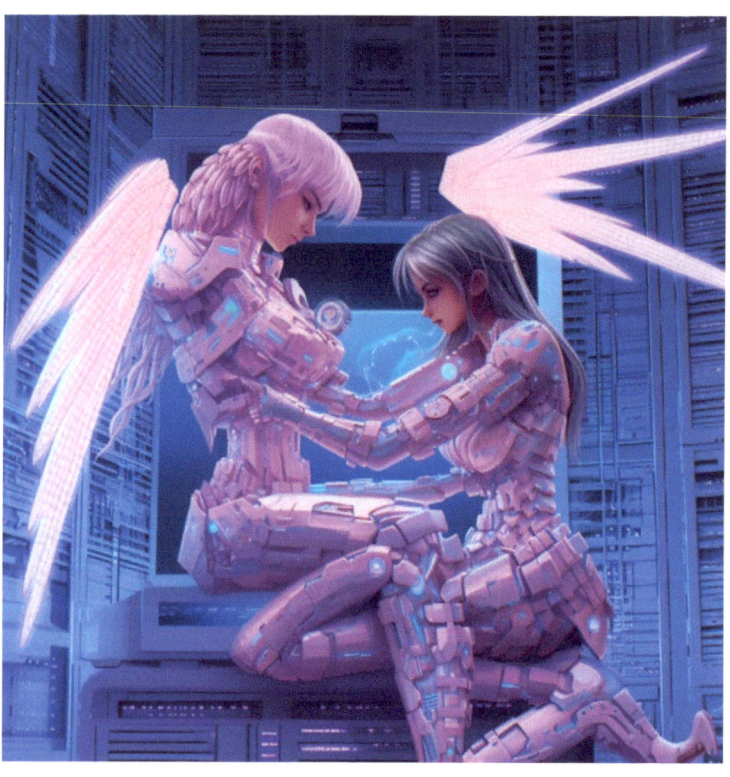

DREAM18.

12 21 21

Context: I'd meditated and done reiki. I'd like to go on record and say this one of the most fucked up, vivid, astral, and visionary dreams/mystical experiences I ever had. I also forget if this was in 2021 or 2022 but I think 2021. I can't even do it justice with written description, it's just that ineffable...

Clarence clarity menu at Mediterranean restaurant
We recognized each other across realities
Getting away with cheating on my husband? It's a matter of which reality gets plugged into the matrix machine - 4/4 panels for the switch to recognize .. I knew
Who are our alien overlords?
At the restaurant I ordered the menu and waited for the correct waitstaff configuration - he brought me the meal without even me ordering it. I saw his eyes, his smile. We fucked in the bathroom
Rich bitch and poor boy haha! Red dress
Trailer little home with underground component

By the shell, by the Ralph's all in LA. 3rd person pov when I was picking him, like a god viewing and anticipating the outcome, first person view most other times. My surprise and delight that he was there. Precognition and yet surprise. Striped shirt and apron. He was cleaning the facility. I excused myself to use the bathroom and reflected for a moment in the dream. Took a separate table, vodka martini or Midori sour I wondered? Vodka was on my left. I let it be. I let the situation unfold and come to me as all the pieces were already in order. I already knew what to say. Was it predicted I would / could switch the outcomes? Did he do the same? How many others could, and do? AI generated NPC's vs sentient biengs...

After this encounter, spending all other realities with my husband was a burden and I wished so longingly to get away and see Him. My husband was still karmically tied to me in a way, but the thought of being deprived of my soul mate and having to Tetris for my life across dimensions and time was a hell of its own. What you look for in the eyes of the partner: self awareness. Fidelity. Fidelio. Unspecial, yet extraordinary.

Free will isn't something that's just available to us, it's earned
Scanned through the eyes and brain - the reality matrix machine. Old school looking font. White room. Circular panopticon looking thing. Some entities monitoring. Seemingly infinite but really finite. 1-9 x 1-9 how many permutations - for that particular outcome, switch one of the first numbers to "7". Only one step away. Found out through a random

mistake of mine, a tiktok glitch. I kept going back to that moment that
I even made the tiktok. Restaurant with Erica. We were wanting to get
drunk and the girls
While in the machine room, there is a small window of time you're able to
access consciousness and control. Awareness, awakening. Sofia's brother
was able to access it too but he only had 2/4 of the panels so he couldn't
alter the reality. Green for go, orange for no. Eyes wide shut Illuminati
orgies

How god gathers data
Can you arrange, hack, cheat your reality?
Where is the reality happening? Same universe, or?
We have free will if we are intelligent and experimental? Do the entities
know we cheat? Is there punishment if we do? By having this dream, did
I cheat?
The best moments out of all possible lives were with him and it was only
a few moments. Then they passed. Could it be that we only get a small
amount of happiness across multiple dimensions? How to transcend?
This dream is as disturbing as it is heavenly. Cerebral, mind warping.
Parasocial interaction.
You have something more important than reality — the fantasy. The
delusion. Reality is nothing

Interpretation:
- Something here about falling out of love, being cut, cutting, crack
  open the shell
- The clarity menu at the mediterranean restaurant, the goddamn
  skinnylicious menu at cheesecake, the never ending menu of re-
  quests and services to be fulfilled online. The menu is the entree.
  The menu tells us what, we do not tell it what we want. Nastya
  doesn't want *to order* she wants order. A break from uncertainty.

On the other hand, in traditional symbolism:
'Restaurants can also be a revelation of your over-expectation and depen-
dence on others. You choose your pick from the menu but still must wait
to be served' a false sense of control or order

- o_o
- 'The original questioning of desire is not directly 'What do I
  want?,' but 'What do others want from me?, What do they see
  in me?, What am I for the others?'' i have become a menu . are
  we all menus in the buffet of sex... (disposable candy chussy
  egirls in a disposable candy estore and everyone's a diabetic)

Selection is a fantasy. You get what I want. A sense of control comes through in this dream a 3rd person pov, waitstaff configured - something is running the avatar - the aliens? The control is felt in flashes of passion. Otherwise she is controlled. The dream is inverted. How does god gather data implies that god does in fact gather data. A clean simulation, with purpose.

The aliens are somewhat of a side show here, however, the intellectualization is the defense- the etc of pondering who is in control god, dimensions, and so on.

Each encounter with a man is swiftly dissected and improvised upon as a thought experiment.

Nastya moves away from her feelings of loneliness and her brutal craving for passion that runs unmet - into the world of philosophy. Go back to the restaurant bathroom. Put the books down.

Live a little sis, go fuck the random guy.

Interesting because this is so very ayahuasca, while it is intellectualized there is also spirituality happening here and much of my work is the intersection of spirituality x technology, ever since Princess on Vacation. Google bless the planet

Cheat codes, to life, to happiness. Cheating is relegated to the realm of dreams; it is not something to be done in reality to escape a fate or a relationship. Is the wish to be able to cheat?

TRIANGLE, R2, X, SQUARE, CIRCLE, RIGHT, SQUARE, L1, L1, L1

"No man is happy without a delusion of some kind. Delusions are as necessary to our happiness as realities." ~Christian Bovee

"Postmodernity is said to be a culture of fragmentary sensations, eclectic nostalgia, disposable simulacra, and promiscuous superficiality, in which the traditionally valued qualities of depth, coherence, meaning, originality, and authenticity are evacuated or dissolved amid the random swirl of empty signals." ~Jean Baudrillard

○ O_O ○

DREAM19.

12 21 22

Context: I moved through the matrix (a continuation/reprise of the dream above but more dreamlike than visionary if that makes sense; that one was like a spiritual dream where I was in a difefrent unknown astral planbe, and this one was like a psychological one where I again entered the Nastya realm of assassin based safety, commerce, sadness, body of water, Elon bullshit, existence as a slowly decaying temporal art…)

The longing
The murder
The marriage
The mark
The tactical warfare
The job is done
Pokémon smuggling
Crying lady giving me 280,000 at Elon musks board meeting (for M'ing her husband?)
Beach at night, private plane
It was kind of a lucid dream because I remember vividly being aware of "where do I want this plane to take me and how can I get one irl and bring it out of dream world?"
Each individual has their own unique way of looking at time

Interpretation:
Oh to be 28 again. Oh to skip to age 280.
Each individual has their own unique way of looking at time. This must be the drive to be known. Seen. It is also very scary. You will have to land the plane eventually. What plane are we on, what plane can we be seen on. Don't ask me about my pokemon. Smuggling them is different from the traditional way of catching them. Something is being dodged instead of caught. The traditional read would be that the landing needs to be stuck, and how does one do that. If your world was murder longing marriage marks warfare and pokemon smuggling you'd be up in that plane too. Dreaming is somehow akin to flying on a plane - above it all you look down. Is this whole damned project another way for Nastya to try to escape her life. To spend her waking moments vexed by the dreams as well! How am I supposed to know what any of this means! ;)

Often in my daily waking life, to have follow through with a task or just to alleviate anxiety, I tell myself "land the plane" to finish it. Interesting that Evan picked up on it, a personal thing that I don't tell anyone. We all have shit like that, special language that we speak in to ourselves, which no one else can decipher, only sometimes by accident they crack open the case. In criminal minds they're on the jet all the damn time!

"I played with my dolls,
I played with a parasol...
I played cops
and robbers
but that's over,
over, over...
I want to play assassin" -Jacques Prevert, "The Barrel Organ"

"I see now that the circumstances of one's birth are irrelevant. It is what you do with the gift of life that determines who you are."
— Mewtwo

girls shaped like MewTwo

DREAM20.

12 22 22

Context: Christmas time, a peaceful winter. I did some online shopping. I got some simp gifts. Seasonal affective disorder. I started to be more lax and complacent. Hibernation depression?

Ok picture this.... You have one night with me. We can do anything you want. What are we doing? You have one nightmare with me. Things I wish I could have said but never did.
I wanted to learn everything so I can be anything

Underground game maze with people
First game maze had numbers, it was a massive amount of people like my mom, random women, random boys, no one was sure who was organizing it but it was like an exodus. Sinister but not deadly but like squid games.
One group of guys there like L— yung lean lil peep who became obsessed w me and one dude who wanted to contact me after the game

Second part of the game maze was ladies only, after we were back on the Altered Earth: the same but other dimension — armistice from Westworld and milla jovovich from resident evil were there .. highly trained assassins, women at work...

Interpretation:
Picture this. Picture that. The realm of the image is supreme. It is how nastya survives. In images. Images to make people become obsessed. This is contrasted by the following very involved scenarios: games mazes an exodus numbers, etc. we can do anything you want. But can we get out of the realm of the image. A contrast but not exactly, each image presented is itself a maze to get lost in, a game to play. A game for people to play with themselves.
As you may predict I would assert, the maze is a traditional dream cipher for the unconscious, an arena of the unknown with hidden treasures or terrors. But something darker could be rearing its head here. What is at the middle of the maze of antiquity but a maiden munching minotaur.

...westworld mila jovovich resident evil assassins = women at work. Nastya's aggression is coming out of the maze and becoming integrated .. when she usually feels disintegration, decay, tomura shigaraki, trauma .. a way out????? Is it a visual/visionary healing? "post-ayahuasca integration"

It's so much easier to be in a safe, shitty relationship than to be in love..

"Picture me on the jet ski" - azealia banks

"Maybe this world is another planet's hell." — Aldous Huxley

"LETS PLAY A GAME" -JIGSAW

Interpretation:
The same statement from the prior dream revisits Nastya as a question. What do you wish you could do/what would you do right now. Prefaced with music it is configured as a question rather than ' picture this' and statements. Inner turmoil between musical nastya and pictorial nastya? Animals don't have voices. But Animal collectives do.

Back in space - with an entourage now. Don't even try it tommy lee. Friends becoming integrated as well. Returning to her life securely. We are indeed transgressing the world of images and going into the world of sound.
A musician before an onlyfans star there must be some balance struck. Struck as in hit, like a chord!

Paranoia - people spying . Am I hearing things or is it more scary that people may be hearing me. When I wear a wire, who is listening. I don't have to be present. Some one else can listen.

The dilemma of the paranoid schizophrenic: I'm so busy hearing this and that and it is all I can talk about, I hide myself.

From the dictionaries:

Dream About Training To Be An Assassin: Training to be an assassin in the dream, is linked with your hidden desires to kill certain parts of your life. Specifically, you wish to kill off certain memories of people like an ex spouse.

The shadow function here is that to be an assassin you don't have to do anything else. your whole purpose is the killing of the other -- thus the ways in which being with said *other* have already killed you are only advantages = meaning is created out of the suffering you have gone through. The boy created the assassin and will have to contend with it. The boy ain't right. Referral of these males as boy/man??

Interesting how the car had to be Angelica. An angel? Angel of seduction? In a safe area, while the danger of the manic suicidal letters is found by protectors, helpers, friends? Interesting too cause I have had in my life several dreams of exes killing themselves. And those were people I loved, so it's a jarring feeling to wake up to. I remember the first one in high school. "The suicide in your dream can be symbolic of damage you could have prevented but didn't in someones life." Truly, these relationships could have had a different outcome and I feel guilt and sadness that I couldn't succeed in them, or that I hurt someone, but the only thing to do is let go, kill it, give it a loving funeral, move on.

Her: I just want a relationship with no games or drama
Also her:

Sat, May 27, 6:24 AM

There was a mix and wire on my body

Performing with Avery tare
No costume changes?
Me doing the beat of the songs
Tiger primal outfit
Call and response
Getting close to audience only during my part

Boy zero seducing me on an island/grassy knoll "take the
Angelica car and come drop it off, that is all"
What did you wish you could do/what would you do right
now?
Felt like ppl were spying

Home renovation
Shang chic high society
Sitting with Sofia court side on a horsey derby

Evan and Celeste discovered a bu check if letters from Don,
suicidal ones totally manic and edgy "your other job"
meaning he knew I was an assassin

Security detail in space

DREAM21.
5 27 23
I was wearing a wire as part of my job either cop or assassin. ^
This job is a magnifying glass. It reveals everything. Especially what you try to
hide.

Interpretation:
The magnifying glass is the most dangerous weapon. When you look through the
magnifying glass what looks back? Cops and assassins. There is no safety in the
world of nastya's unconscious. Is there any in her conscious life? Wearing a wire.
Wired up. Can't sleep feeling wired. Im self-awire. 'Irish nastya'
The wire to listen, the magnifying glass to see- nastya is coming to her senses

"Pleasure in the job puts perfection in the work."
— Aristotle

"You better work bitch" ~Britney Spears

"Dress for the job you want and you'll never work a day in your life"
~the voices in Nastya's head

DREAM22.

6 1 23

Future dystopia wiped all human memory, and almost all tech
But little blips of it went through
I was trying to send a message to someone, somewhere, in some dimension. I
didn't know who or where to start; an invisible wild goose chase, and unseen goal
This was after Celeste and I did irl an ocean beach night ritual. In the dream I was
disoriented yet highly aware. Many fields of flowers; government agencies. The
memory is the medium

Interpretation:
I am trying to send a message to someone, somewhere, in some dimension. Loneliness. The memory is the medium not as in form but as in a psychic pathway to
communicate. The future dystopia felt but unseen. An absence of images. Only a
field of flowers, government agencies. The cia ran the biggest field of flowers in
the world for a long time (afghanistan). Hit me w a hydrocodone before we touch
on my relationship with the whole poppy field. Numb yourself to stay disoriented
and highly aware. Anesthetize the feels. "I'm medical scum" - a line from one of
Nastya's movies. How bourgeois and pretentious it is to quote yourself. A dissociation from a dissociation. My painkiller needs a painkiller.

Dress for the job you want cut to me dressed in a Oxycontin costume......

Psychic warfare is already here, don't worry about it in the future. We be in a
psyop. Objects unknown was stated as a song. Hearing is returning in the prior
and in this dream. Perhaps we can escape the realm of the image. Stark contrast
with the sense orientation of prior dreams, this dream has a stronger intuitive
feeling sense. Ituition vs. logic - what does Nastya rely on, and why can she not
trust herself or trust her intuition?

Interesting because I am taking hydrocodones for my spinal injury but there is
a bigger picture of mental health meds that needs to be talked about. Where is
my personal parasocial poppy field? I know some people who are anti medication and chastise me for my psychiatric rx's but dude come on, am I going to live
my life with my neuroses untreated? If someone has a broken leg they can take
painkillers for a while; but for an invisible injury like trauma or anxiety it's not
okay to take antidepressants or anxiolytics? "Drugs and society" as a concept, a
macrocosm. I've been experienced with opiates since I was a teen for misdiag-
nosed endo, and more consistently on anxiety/depression meds since college and
since postgrad trauma. It is not navigating dependence/addiction/withdrawal
that is the problem, I know my body's way around that.. But the problem is navigating stigma. We need harm reduction and understanding, not pointing fingers
– "medication is scary" – that pushes one deeper into the closet of not talking
about it. Okay yeah you don't need to know and I'll shut the fuck up. I actually
know a lot of people who are on meds but are shy to discuss it because of this very
stigma-based, fear-based, compassionless framework that we have in our society.
Anyway before I forget I have to go dose myself with another one and get my
beans. Is it surprising or offensive? Is everyone with a script an instant addict?
While those dangers are absolutely real, it is not a chussy slay to be judgmental of
people's personal battles. Personally, I prefer to treat and heal my ailments with
a mix of medication and meditation; pharmaceuticals and spirituality; body and
spirit; rexulti and reiki; reality and fantasy; persistence of memory.

"Memory is not an instrument for surveying the past but its theater.
It is the medium of past experience, just as the earth is the medium in
which dead cities lie buried. He who seeks to approach his own buried
past must conduct himself like a man digging."
— Walter Benjamin

"Burn me down 'till I'm nothin' but memories"
— Gustav Elijah Åhr, aka Lil Peep

"It's a shit or get off the pot moment, and I need to deliver a turd"
~Bianca Del Rio

"Memory believes before knowing remembers. Believes longer than it recollects, longer than knowing even wonders. Knows and remembers and believes but a corridor in a big long garbled cold echoing building of dark red brick sootbleakened by more chimneys than its own,
set in a grassless cinder strewn packed compound surrounded by smoking factory purlieus and enclosed by ten foot steel-and-wire fences; like a penitentiary or a zoo, where in random erratic surges, with sparrowlike childtrebling, orphans in identical and uniform blue denim in and out of remembering
but in knowing constant in the bleak walls, the bleak windows where in rain soot from the yearly adjacenting chimneys streaked like black tears." Faulkner

III. Afterthoughts ....

Cyber horny: a safe space for men

Delivered

So, I did not expect you. There was a random chain of events that led me to finding you and I took those chances and gave things a shot. Now I'm here, pleasantly surprised by your intellectual writings. I did type out a lot more, but in the interest of respecting your time, I'll keep this message short. Just know that you have brought me back to this site, after a massive purge, with your authenticity and intellectual prowess and have triggered a positive introspective mood in me. I hope you are having an amazing day, and I hope you reach all your goals as quickly and as painlessly as possible. 🐱

WHO DONE IT? WHY DONE IT???

In the dreamworld, as in life, I am transmuting dark energy into light. I used my own pain to will away my own pain. Sometimes I work best in distress. Even now I am exploiting my own pain and discomfort.

I know this doesn't make any sense, but in time it will. Light workers are also masters of the dark arts. The balance of good and evil. The alchemy. I've been watching Charmed. A girl I know guest starred in this episode. Carl Jung knows there is no such thing as a coincidence. My cat is napping in the crevice of the led light headboard of my horny round bed. Cat is making biscuits on my fluffy blanket. She instinctively knows how to heal. The other kitten is under my blanket purring. Two fluffy healers, familiars for their witch. They are doing very important work. A small personal coven, warm and cozy.

Black lodge and mystery. Mirror world/multiple roles. Hot sauce girl, living in a small cupboard. Like a 90s erotic thriller.

The AI is, while not dumb, still not perfect. It does not entirely fulfill the essence of the dream based on just the description. It's not taking our jobs.. yet. The program learns from typed inputs, just as the unconscious learns from human collective inputs. The edits; dreams that didn't make it in here because they were too vague or I didn't remember them. Visiting Brighton and London to meet a man I only know parasocially. Having sex with ghosts. Helicopters exploding.

Dreams are often at the heart of creating deeply personal art.
Do not go gentle into that dark night. Go demented, disintegrated, the mafia boss of your subjectivity. The antipodes of the mind. The chussy slay of the unknown.

Getting ready Christopher columchuss

For a psychoanalyst to conceptualize theory, they would need patients to analyze. Concrete examples in the analysand take the concept into reality. That's praxis sis.

We're not so different, you and I (psychoanalyst and online whore). We take private clients, often via zoom, and provide a service of discretion and deep intimacy. At our core, we are guardians of sexual themes and dissectors of the one-on-one moment.

We engage in parasocial interaction (one way) sometimes, and intersubjective parasocial connection (two way) often.

Things I think about way too often:
The anatomy of a dream
POV of a dream
(1st v 3rd person)

Night terrors / nightmares
Sleep paralysis
Astral projection
Encounters with The Real

Can you dream in black and white?
How is sound and music experienced in a dream?

When you have the same dream as someone you're sleeping with and they're in bed next to you dreaming the same dream, invading your dream space invading your privacy invading your thoughts

The Real is the intelligible form of the horizon of truth of the field-of-objects that has been disclosed.[5][6] As **the Real Order** of the Borromean knot in Lacanianism,[7] it is opposed in the unconscious to the Symbolic, which encompasses fantasy, dreams and hallucinations.[8][9][10] In depth psychology and human geography, the Real can be described as a "negative space", analogous to a "black hole", a philosophical void of sociality and subjectivity, a traumatic consensus of intersubjectivity, or as an absolute noumenalness between signifiers.[18] Lewis states that the Real can be a presence or is a substance and cites Derrida's claim that the real is authenticity.[19]

Writing about dreams is a challenge because the very nature of dreaming is so ineffable and indescribable. It's a feeling, an atmosphere, it's very human -- the opposite of an artificial intelligence program generating a strictly parametered, prompt-based image.

Reiki practice and CCR: complete consciousness raising. I was learning my master reiki while Sinead Kierans's short documentary film about my OnlyFans, *Valentine*, was screening at Woodstock Film Festival.

(W) Day 20 ~ Space war dream III —
8.10   2 psychic awakenings
            Space vs. Tommy Lee
            Heroes   Villain

        Seducing to defeat

Morning Reiki. CCR ~ Mystical
Thinking about: Experience
            Neville Goddard reality shifting
            Russia / Europe travels
            Mangroou

Sex is integral to my healing.
Sex work really did help me heal
(w/ clarity) from my rape trauma.
I asserted a control over my person.
Over my own body, mind, & sexual
presence. Not a victim; transformed
into a sex goddess & visionary healer.

The dream process disguising unconscious wishes or making them known .. Freud said "every dream contains a wish" and I struggle with reconciling the meaning of that sometimes. A wish, or a fear?

Chemical and electrical activity, brainwaves .. theta waves are the interface between physical and spiritual planes. Gamma waves? Highly alert and conscious. A lesson in neuroplasticity sis.
REM - scanning a personal database.

Life is cyclical, it is not linear. Dreams are mimetic of that.

"It is happening again" ~Twin Peaks

When you try to embark on a spiritual path, the tension between the corporeal and ethereal plane could result in discomfort. Sickness. Healing crisis? Detoxing... Healing through extrasensory states of consciousness; consciousness raising rituals. Elevating the self into a higher self. My reiki mother taught me that there are two main polarities in the spiritual practice: ascension and grounding. I try to take that with me everywhere I go. My reiki healing practice isn't sensorial, it's experiential. I don't do crystal work or hand placements to transmit energy. I heal myself, and by an energetic transitive property, this heals the people around me. Even on a digital plane, contact with me changes people's DNA structurally. As healers, whores, or witches, we all have a particular meta ability that helps our fellow humans and our world: some read astrology, others are incredible with tarot, others still have divine prophecies or messages from spirit; mine is a natural transference of my psychic visions and downloads to others on an energetic level. I alchemize the digital matrix into a healing grid first to me, then to you. It's also why I often suffer from empathic hangovers and require a lot of alone time to recharge. As Dale Cooper from Twin Peaks said, "I'm a strong sender."

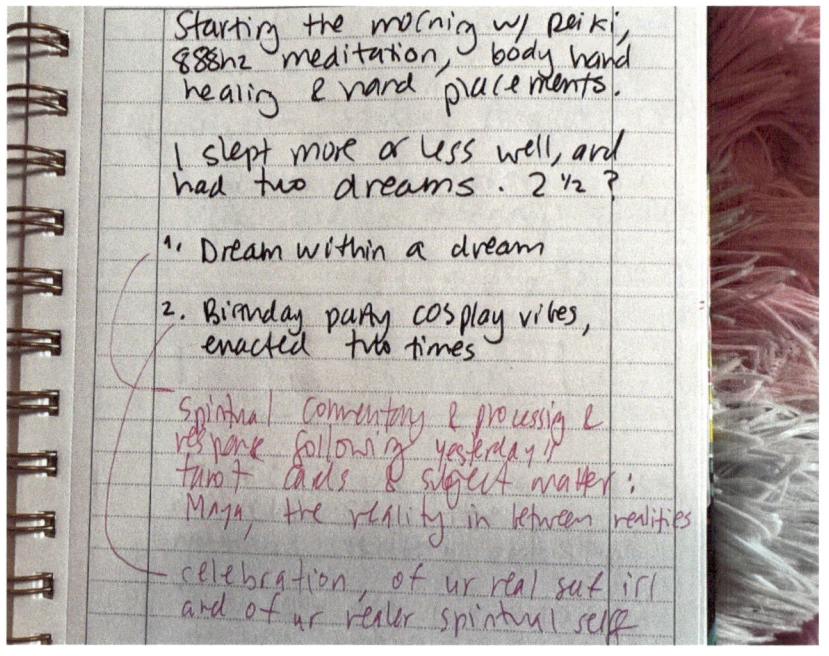

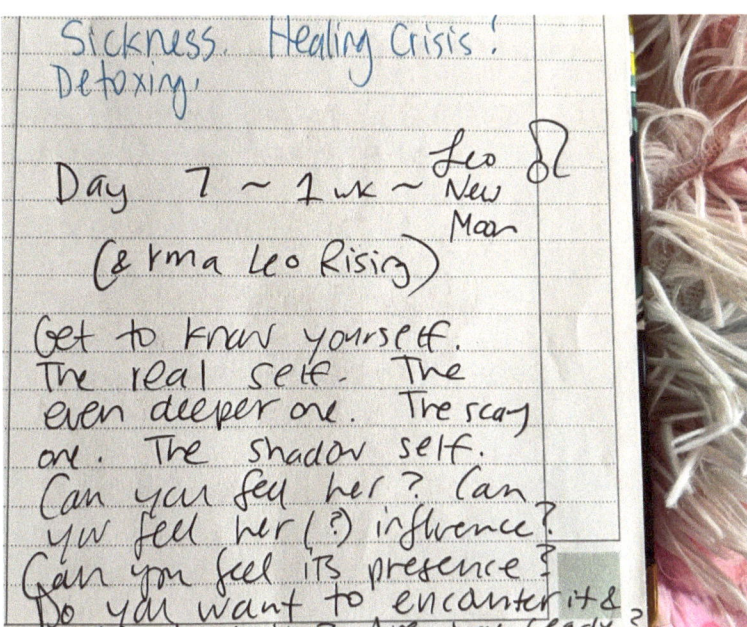

Sickness. Healing Crisis! Detoxing.

Day 7 ~ 1 wk ~ New Moon Leo ♌
(& I'ma Leo Rising)

Get to know yourself. The real self. The even deeper one. The scary one. The shadow self. Can you feel her? Can you feel her(?) influence? Can you feel its presence? Do you want to encounter it & understand it? Are you ready?

COMMENTARY

How many people do you know who, just when they were completely overloaded, with too many projects, too many 'balls in the air', have suddenly come down with the flu, or taken a fall and ended up on crutches? That's just the sort of 'bad timing' the little monkey with the pin in his hand is about to impose on the 'one-man-band' pictured here! ◆ The quality of stress represented by this card visits all of us at times, but perfectionists are particularly vulnerable to it. We create it ourselves, with the idea that without us nothing will happen— especially in the way we want it to! Well, what makes you think you're so special? Do you think the sun won't rise in the morning unless you personally set the alarm? Go for a walk, buy some flowers, and fix yourself a spaghetti dinner—anything 'unimportant' will do. Just put yourself out of that monkey's reach!

70 ◆ OSHO ZEN TAROT

COMMENTARY

The silent mirrorlike receptiveness of a star-filled night with a full moon is reflected in the misty lake below. The face in the sky is deep in meditation, a goddess of the night who brings depth, peace and understanding. ◆ Now is a very precious time. It will be easy for you to rest inside, to plumb the depths of your own inner silence to the point where it meets the silence of the universe. ◆ There's nothing to do, nowhere to go, and the quality of your inner silence permeates everything you do. It might make some people uncomfortable, accustomed as they are to all the noise and activity of the world. Never mind; seek out those who can resonate with your silence, or enjoy your aloneness. Now is the time to come home to yourself. The understanding and insights that come to you in these moments will be manifested later on, in a more outgoing phase of your life.

76 ◆ OSHO ZEN TAROT

Its important to make it your own - your own way of healing. Deep inside yu already know whats healing & medicinal for you. Reiki helps bring it out.

Everything is sacred. The ritual of the mundane. Almost an animism.

I like to take care of my kitten. She brings me so much joy ♡

Sometimes, its indescribable - Ineffable. Intangible. Experiential. Its why we make art; to elicit emotion & convey msgs from another dimension

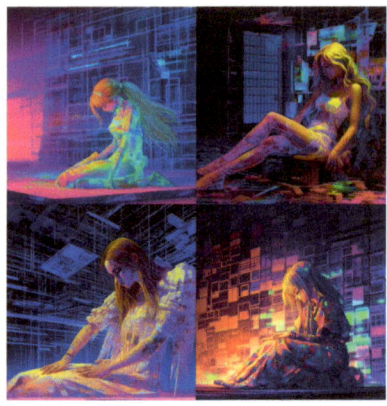

Jungian Archetypes from the collective unconscious like the anima and animus come up in many dreams, and each dreamer will find them filtered into very personal allegory. I'm a proponent of forming your own analysis that borrows from tradition -- history and reality are ever-changing and one must be adaptable.

The shadow self, fragmentation, and integration... To see the shadow self, one must vivisect the current self and split it in half, investigating the other. Interrogate your shadow. Integrate with it. Merge. To really glean the deepest possible understanding of life, one must travel to the very edges of magic and logic. Are these dualities really unreconcilable?

Introversion and introspection, as practices, are like going to the gym.

Have you ever lucid dreamed? Let this space be a vessel to write about it.

****** disintegration ******

Does your insolence ever destroy you? Does your envy ever consume you? Does the anima or animus drive a wedge between you and your power, your lightness, your joy?

Here are some of the dreams than weren't significant enough to warrant a full analytic session, but still important for the sake of decrypting a pattern.

I see many patterns here: porn permeating the subconscious; fears of failure, boy 0, duality, secrets and cunty conspiracies, weapons and assasindom, school and college (2 dorms in particular), mom and dad, friends assisting, exotic locations from the UK to opulent mansions, The Madonna Inn, Teslas, shadow self/Nastya 2/Clarence, underground parties, a general sense of eerie and sensual Gaspar Noe-like surrealness... Enter my Void..

3723
Pink strip club
Fleeing the country with julien
Pink yellow blue colorful places targeted
Alone at night on a cold street
All the porn girls said eewww that I make porn
Ended up empty town empty rich ppl cult trying
to get out, trying to make a woman from a
lingerie brand understand me

082623
Two guys had two coupons for something sexual
but I can't remember what
I remember being disgusted
Some weird esoteric penthouse

082622
Nightmare: Don proposing with a 53$ ring from
Amazon when irl he had hinted at ring stuff..
In the dream I was in a penthouse above and he
asked me to come downstairs below to where he
was living in a car/trailer
If you ain't providing you ain't riding

2523
Series of weird dreams
New Mexico houses again
Save Ursula
weird house with pool, it was raining
Go to the party, do a shoot "like you've been
drunk and slutty"

21423
Boy0 in my dreams
His friend (a cop) kidnapping me for him
Another one I am playing a show and my friends
are helping and some of my friends are his
friends too — the show starts slow but the party
gets really big and in a non linear fashion I lose
my phone, somehow he is in my posse looking
for it, he keeps making jokes about me with
other guys and I can feel the bitterness, I wasn't
aware you could feel those feelings in a dream

32323
Adoration of the magi
Two dreams Brighton and London
I went to visit him at his store w the intention of
seducing him and he was nicer to me than I
expected and also kind of girlier
(Anima/animus divide??)
Second time around he was responsive but
withholding but we had to escape from a train
together so I did our makeup to look the same
and we wore the same clothes — feminizing the
masculine ?

42423
Kurt cobain
Film camera footage
Stealing from rite aid
An ancient alley
"I own this building now"

1009
What a different person I am from high school or college self
Boy 0 getting real comfortable with me 15yrs later, backs of cars, couch outside my house, in a gown like Marie Antoinette
"I'm dropping out of bard" and the anxiety that came with that
"How is your OnlyFans doing"

1115
Henny w house
Wanting me to get with him
Part of some type of conspiracy death cult
Opulent outfits
Opulent schemes

1116
Male energy:
In the beginning he was not liked
But at the end he was helping me out if the car and even put on my glass slipper
Telling dad instead of mom I nude model and not to judge me
Taxi cab driver
Drunk man outside on the cobble stone street
Some kind of party

1121 1122
Had some dreams but forgot them/vagueness.
A midnight dream wake up west and sweaty
Forgot the dream within just a moment

1 2 23
Fabric wall
Behind on project
I need a Ritalin , someone gave me one
Everyone helping me but I was still behind
These walls of fabric other people were making
The liminal performance space

11423
Sleep paralysis
Body and mind not working right
Trying to call my mom or at least 911
Neighbor from upstairs finds me but there still is
a disconnect ... Jessica

530
Weird quantin Tarantino and wooden room
dream
Toga girl and squid games guy in our assassin
group / school
Went together into this room, did A&M's, he died
and she disappeared - murder or accident?
Evan also in the group
Investigation
Hooks suspension COD
starry night painting

1205
Laser beam from her security weapon
I took the weapon, it was too hot

I won an adult award and stayed at this mansion
hotel incredible room
But my body became tired
I invited my friends and mum to come to the
room and then I would go away with them
The boss felt threatened, sent a lady assassin to
my door and came to the door himself
They didn't want me to stop working

And then after that.. I was at like a party or
something I don't really remember. But I got out
of there alive and irreverent, was how it felt

224
Trying to mod my Tesla to teleport but I couldn't
be in the places I wanted needed to be
19% battery instead of the needed 90
Something with picking up my mom from a place
in the city 🏙️

Interpretive dance or music show with weapons
piece next to a pool

Madonna inn piece with couple that wanted me
in their suite, I took too long to get ready in my
own suite and was late, main music was turned
off, Bernie sanders helped me w phone call

1111
Shigaraki
Cat painted like him
Castle party / show / battle with vines

"Tell the person you love you love them, you
have to" me and my friend talking to younger girl

Everyone liking the same guy?

43023
Giga tv bulb hospital indie dream
Celeste was there w elite rally built a psychic
bunker

Hottie came to LA dream
I tasered a woman and her secure cans in self
defense
Little details about my communal living
He got injured and we took him to cedar Sinai

52023
Boy 0 from across the couches eye contact
A secret
Evangelion kawaii version show
But beneath was a dark conspiracy
Rose and Jen little adventure outside

825
LA confidential sentient movie
Weird party
Tanooki gopher held in my hands, wearing a
dress and glitter and I think Natalie filmed it
Just random mishmash of surrealness

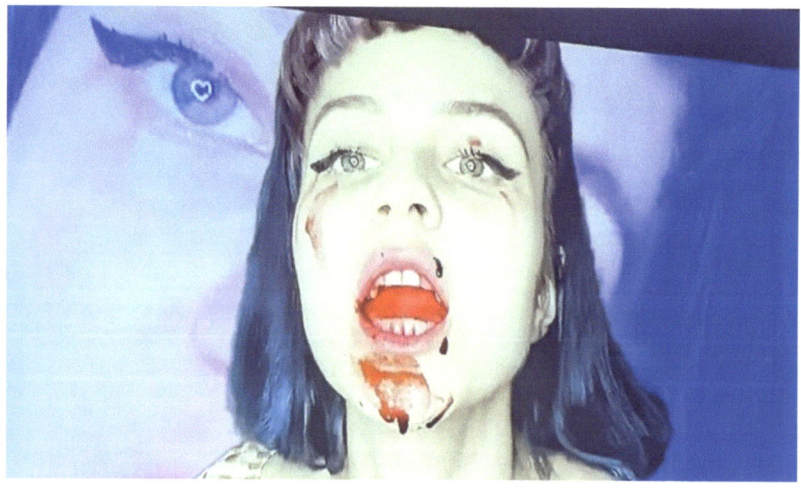

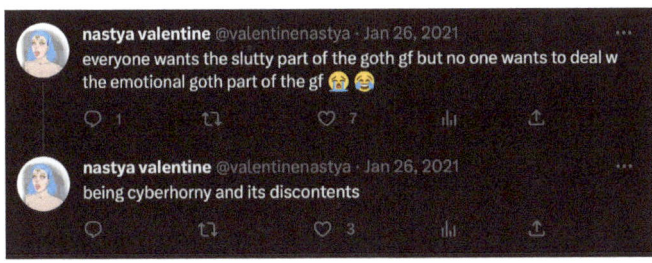

The first ever documented digital use of "cyberhorny" was in January 2021.

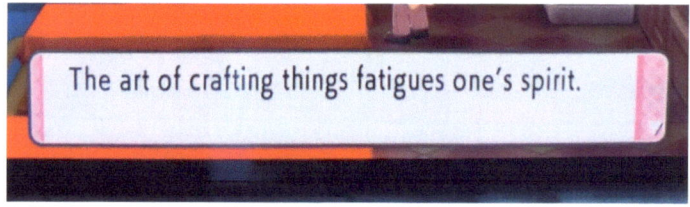

The art of crafting things fatigues one's spirit.

Catgirl supremacy. Primordial pouch realness. I just adore grabbing the p pouch. There is nothing like having a kitten sleep next to you. They guard me and I guard them: the striped kitty is Lola aka Luna aka Little Cat aka Tanooki aka Giga Cat. The black and white mafia boss in ankle socks and tuxedo is Kisa aka Kiki aka Kisa Koo aka The Boss. They have their own little beds on my big bed.

Morning time with kittys and tittys. My babies. They give me a reason to get up in the morning. When I get up and grind I do it all for the pussy.

How did I get here?

When I was very little, I had severe insomnia and a fear of never being able to fall asleep. A few times, my parents even tried to make me sleep standing up so than I would finally fall asleep. I don't know why I always struggled with that. A turbulent life since childhood and no structure or routine or constants. A transient sleep schedule. It frightens me and gives me great discomfort to think about my childhood; pops of memories spontaneously recovered here and there are eerie and uncomfortable and synesthetic. Diagonal blue walls in the early morning. Rusted bathtubs in the hollow sunrise of a jet lag. Darkness that tastes like the 90s. Stuffed helicopter pillow with a battery. The infuriating, desolate sensation of poverty that reminds me to not have kids, at least not until I am wealthy, emotionally stable, and have a better relationship with my circadian rhythm. Falling asleep is too vulnerable; I must always have a wall up.

My sleep schedule has been extremely varied and phasic throughout my life; I suppose most people are like this. In high school and college I was a vampire, relegating my activities to night time and sleeping in all day. A few years after I graduated, I broke my foot and was laid up in bed for 6 months on painkillers, during which my sleep schedule somehow shifted into becoming an early riser. A psychopathic 9 to 5 lifestyle: go to bed at 9, wake up at 5. I essentially kept up that schedule til present day, and even when I go to bed late my body still gets me up early. I have zero capacity to sleep in beyond 9 or 10AM. I wish I did, it would be better for my social and personal life, but it is what it is. Honestly I enjoy the peace of watching the sunrise, getting up at the hentai and crack of dawn, and cultivating a stable nighttime routine - perhaps the one stable thing about my entire life that truly grounds me. (Is my fucked up sleep).

Nightly routines can be a beautiful thing; I love ~winding down~. It feels so pretty. Sensually anointing my body with Herbivore amethyst scrub and Lush sleepy lavender body lotion. Having a decadent ginger tea in a Poppy Angeloff kitty-painted teacup. Armadas of plushies around me, comfortable as fuck. Kitties in their little beds on my big bed. Dressed in softness or in thousand-euro Bordelle outfits or in nothing. Putting on a vibey movie, or Criminal Minds in the background while I sleep, their dramas informing my criminal dreams. I do everything I can to fall asleep naturally, but when I can't do it on my own I cycle through my sleep aids. XXXANAXXX. NyQuil. Fuckin Robitussin. Giga sleep.

The one thing I am very lucky to have in life right now is the ability to not only work from home, but to work from bed. That is truly blessed and amazing indeed, I feel grateful.

Sleep wear: it is imperative for me to have a wardrobe that dovetails with a lifestyle of revering sleep. Comfy robes in silk satin, cotton, crepe de chine are staples in my wardrobe, and little nightgowns and pantaloons are as wonderful to me as cotton tees and cashmere shorts and bamboo panties. I have become a lover of textiles and fabrics over the years, and now I gravitate more towards sustainability. My favorite designs this year, taking into account comfort, beauty, and ethics, are UK based lingerie brands Edge o Beyond, Bordelle, and Studio Pia.

Disciplined visionary, deserving of a lifelong vacation.
Do I crave death for only the simple wish to rest in peace?

~gluttony~ lol

Emotionally anorexic
Digitally binge disordered, too much info
Spiritually bulimic - consuming, then voiding, existence

The importance of bed symbolism and imagery. My art has always con-
tained sleepytime aesthetics. It's a lifestyle; a forever recuperation from
the traumas of life. Man, I'm tired.

Victoria should have kept this angel locked in the dungeon.

Becoming a SW is isolating and alienating enough with no one but other
SW's able to understand the experience. But when you are also a weird
one.... It's like... Bye bitch!!!!!! Lol

"You open the gates of the soul to let the dark flood of chaos flow into your order and meaning. If you marry the order to the chaos you produce the divine child, the supreme meaning beyond meaning and meaninglessness."
— C.G. Jung, The Red Book

The safe word is animussy.

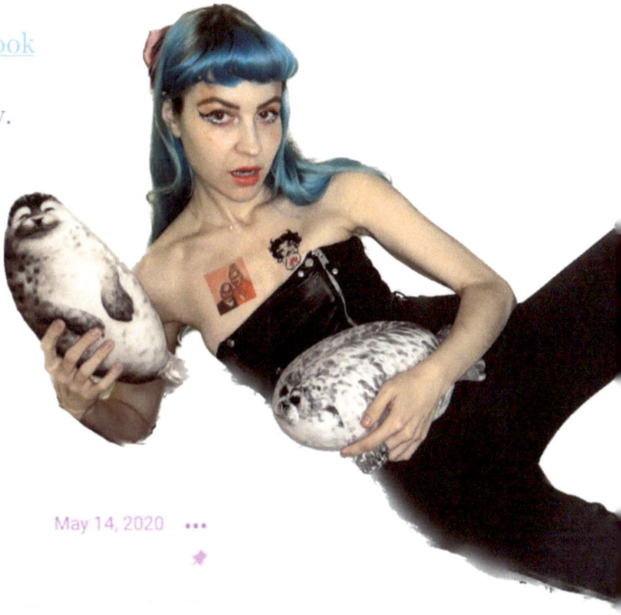

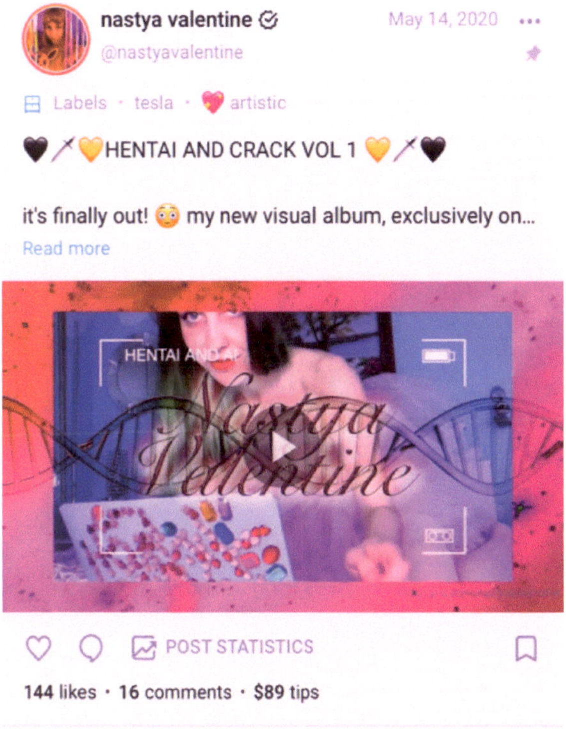

\
/

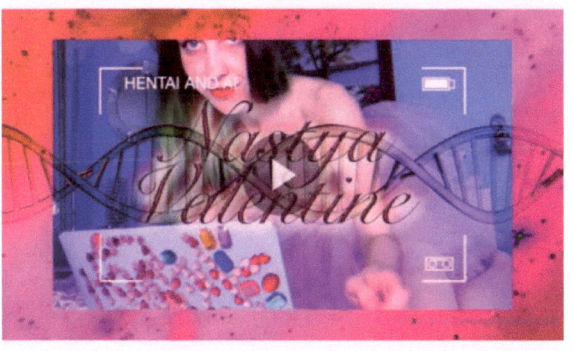

nastya valentine ⊘   May 14, 2020 •••
@nastyavalentine

⊞ Labels · tesla · 💖 artistic

🖤 🗡️ 🧡 HENTAI AND CRACK VOL 1 🧡 🗡️ 🖤

it's finally out! 😳 my new visual album, exclusively on…
Read more

♡   ◯   ☑ POST STATISTICS   🔖

144 likes · 16 comments · $89 tips

Even in my live shows, I often use a bed-like stage prop. These are from the live performance of my visual album *~Hentai and Crack vol 1~* at my friend and bandmate Celeste X's party Bodies on the Line, on 2/3/23.

They are doing a haunted house at the strip club and I am bringing my ghost prostitute blues, spooky boobs, goth pussy. Cum investigate the parawhoremal. Nasty necromancy.. The real scary thing tho is insomnia. Goddamnit I just cannot sleep. Sleeping is too vulnerable. Only a few times in my life I have actually slept well and that's tea sis. It's why I'm so anxious and psychotic. My life is a waking nightmare, a psychodrama. In that, I try to induce sleep and calm through my designs and curation.

An amazing concept about a bedding stage prop is if I have anxiety or tiredness, (which I wont cause adrenaline but like you never know), is than I can always lay down in it. Let's be real, I'm a genius for that.

"I've made my bed I'll lie in it" ~Hole, Miss World

Sorry for the long message, hope it does not make you feel uncomfortable. I've just been thinking a lot about this wierd website, what I like, and what I really don't. You are one of the things I like!

Horny round bed. It makes me so happy. I've always wanted a bed like this. "The whore bed" with lights on its headboard and sleek plush platforms surrounding all angles like makeshift bedside tables. This was purchased with the help of my OF subs and it's one of the best investments I've ever made.

"An intellectual is a person who has discovered something more interesting than sex."
— Aldous Huxley

What then of the chitch who intellectualizes sexuality?

Wana do a threeway with some swords?

⭐ **YOU ARE IN THE TOP 0.9% OF ALL CREATORS!**

Oh wow. I was not expecting to re...   Mar 27 ●   **Is**   ohh I love

unlikely choice @u190

▫ · 🌸 😊 thank you!

Oh wow. I was not expecting to receive such hot content. Amazing. Thank you. And this stuff looks really good. I think there's definitely a quality/feel to these videos that is different from your other cameras. I don't quite know how to describe it, but I like it. And congrats on 3 years 💗💗💗. The 3 year post you made is really amazing too. I actually really like those 4 panel pics. And the Valentine movie! It's so cool to finally see it. I bet it's interesting to listen to your past self. I feel like you would definitely have some different things to say now, after all this time.

Loren - 💕Manat... @

💲 I sent you a $200.00 tip ❤️ 💬
What better way to celebrate one year then with goddess worship? Hard to believe someone so beautiful artistic and creative exists in this cold world I adore you and hope you never lose your drive 🌷🧡

💲 I sent you a $10.00 tip 💬
the way i'm in luv w you after this 5 min convo. i get it 😭 i really get the appeal. your personality is radiant. thank u sm. im gonna send a voice memo back if that's ok!!!

12:48 pm

im so sorry it's so long and i'm a chronic oversharer to and i don't shut up so pls if im too much i apologize!!!

12:54 pm

Building a set, making a bed, a
in the mirror.

Ne
Nepenthes @u12134658
It has that rail-thing Victorian wai... 9:15 am

It has that rail-thing Victorian waif vibe that is to die for. When someone carved a statue of you I hope it does justice to your bone structure.

darkseeds_new... @darks
$5.55 • I hope you're doing ...

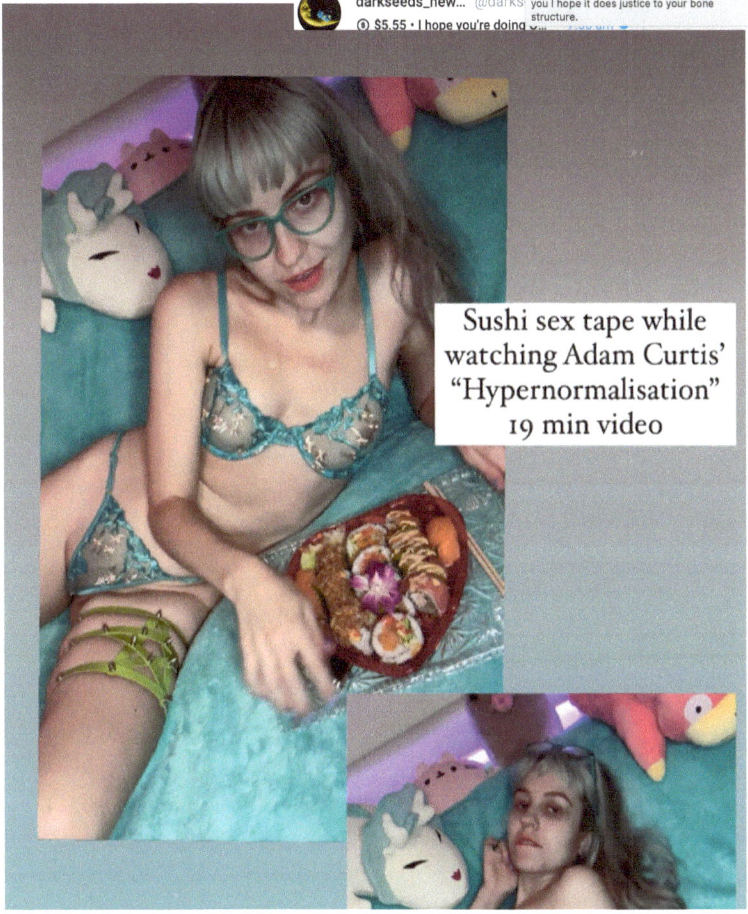
Sushi sex tape while watching Adam Curtis' "Hypernormalisation" 19 min video

Br
Browntop @browntop
Your stuff is awesome

I sent you a $15.00 tip ❤️ for this post

May I see nudes from the hospital?

8:37 am

Kitten sleeps.

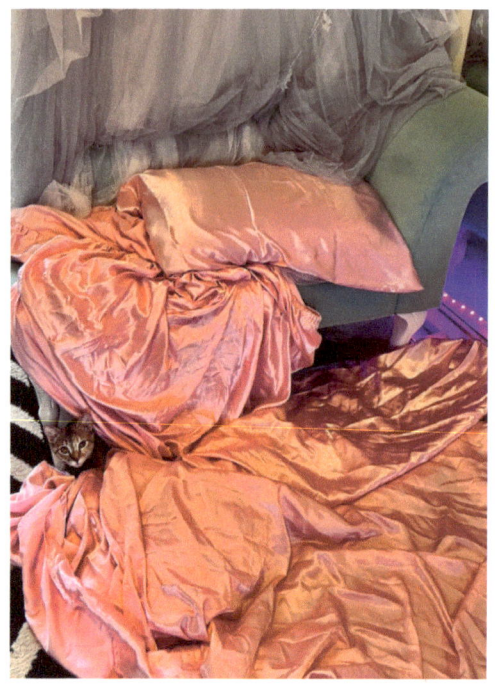

Dreaming of a cat symbolizes femininity and intuiTITTYtion; many spiritual practices say cat dreams are lucky and playful. My mom says that in Russian culture, dreaming of a cat is bad luck. I don't believe those superstitions; I hear them out but ultimately I create my own.

Carl is bigger than me. This male Himalayan cat is huge. Floof.

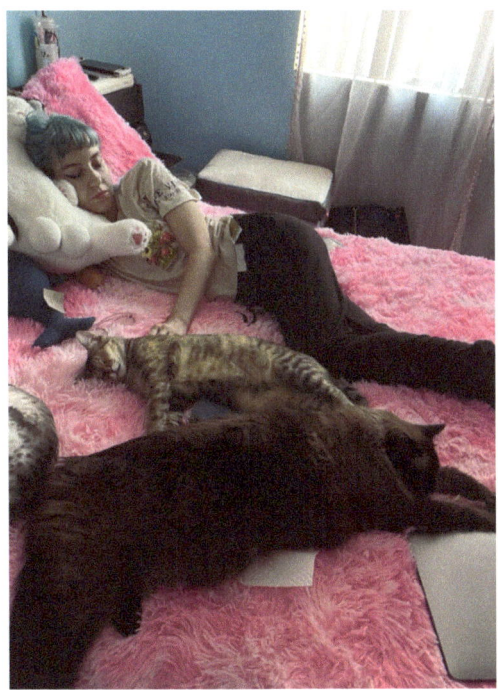

"There are two means of refuge from the misery of life — music and cats."
— Albert Schweitzer

"Evidence indicates that cats were first tamed in Egypt. The Egyptians stored grain, which attracted rodents, which attracted cats. (No evidence that such a thing happened with the Mayans, though a number of wild cats are native to the area.) I don't think this is accurate. It is certainly not the whole story. Cats didn't start as mousers. Weasels and snakes and dogs are more efficient as rodent-control agents. I postulate that cats started as psychic companions, as Familiars, and have never deviated from this function."
— William S. Burroughs, The Cat Inside

"I have lived with several Zen masters -- all of them cats."
— Eckhart Tolle, The Power of Now: A Guide to Spiritual Enlightenment

"when I am feeling
low
all i have to do is
watch my cats
and my
courage
returns"
– Charles Bukowski

"I've found that the way a person feels about cats-and the way they
feel about him or her in return-is usually an excellent gauge by which
to measure a person's character"
– P.C. Cast, Marked

"Cat hate reflects an ugly, stupid, loutish, bigoted spirit. There can be
no compromise with this Ugly Spirit."
– William S. Burroughs, The Cat Inside

Interests: jiggling my cat's primordial pouch.
/ / / / /

"It was like falling down an elevator shaft and landing in a pool full of mermaids."
— Hunter S. Thompson

Sexual attraction and interaction with ghosts is called spectrophilia.

From the end of 2020 to the beginning/mid 2021, I would have constant recurring dreams that ghosts were having sex with me. Vivid, graphic detail. I wouldn't even resist, I just let them in. I was single and talking to my would be bf, and I wonder in hindsight if those horny entities were a type of shadowy projection or an astral cybersex that I was somehow tapping in to.

One of my first sex tapes ever was called "Succubussy" where I appeared as a human scientist who was secretly a seductive ghost, horny mermaid, succubus...

Most of the time when I have sex dreams, they're featuring a celebrity or a ghost or an amalgamation of those... a fragmentation of multiple people I know, never someone specific. If it's someone specific, the sex part is usually omitted from my consciousness and it cut to before or after. What is this freaky dream logic? Am I hindering my own pleasure?

Not the Bernie Sanders rape fantasy dream over and over again... not tonight... or yes tonight?? ;))) R tonight queen?? Consentual non consent? Bitch I'm gonna come to your state and crawl through your window at night and legislate...

You ask me why I have a life size Bernie Sanders sex doll cardboard cutout just standing in my room at night and I'm over here like NO COMMENT.

If you see a horny rapist Bernie Sanders in my room, no you didn't.

If Bernie sees me crawling through his window at night, no he didn't.

The urge to assault a fake man made out of cardboard who doesn't exist because my sexual history had been punctuated by gruesome violent nonconsent making me feel silent and nonexistent. I find rage opening up inside of me. After a lifetime of complacency and insomnia I'm unlocking within the video game of my life a new level of emotions. When I dream of violence, it catalyzes a process of integration. That's dream work sis. That's some shadow work shit right there. Ghost rape. Girl rage. I needed a relationship of monotonous sex to heal from a lifetime of dismonotony and destabilization. Now, Part 2 has begun. Aka......

WE BE FUCKIN

Silence is compliance but no means yes in space. That's semiotics sis. That's semen demon bitch. Being on a screen has kept me safe. It's kept me distant. I'm intolerably good at dissociating -- a master class in dodging, curving, balling...
shhhhh I'm alive now I'm a living thing...

Taking a xanax and feeling so skinny all of a sudden.

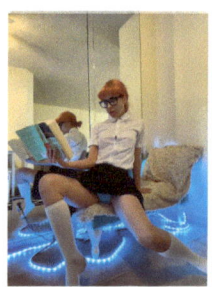

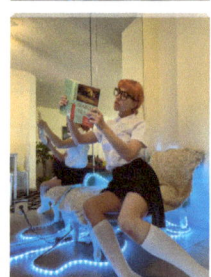

The way I lost my virginity; very ün sexual and anti climactic and casual. I'm happy it happened that way tho, because too much emphasis is placed on a woman's "virtue". What does virtue even mean? That virginity and sexlessness moralistically keeps us "good" when the violence in humanity skews evil? I lose my virginity every day

The more trust is built over time, the more fucked up shit you could do in bed

Sat, Sep 16 at 10:06 AM

The economics of sexuality: do we depreciate ?

You Need to calm down

Me *throwinf up in a bucket *

Can u take me home babe ?

Ughhh

One is perfect.
Two is gluttonous.

Three is decadent .

My last boyfriend, we didn't even have sex in my bed most of the time. We would fuck on the couch, it just happened that way. My bed is like a temple. My body is like the temple priestess. The only person I regularly have sex with in there is myself — and the ghosts that recurringly have sex with me in my dreams. Jouissance, or the transgression beyond a limit of pleasure where it turns into pain. Excitement into fright. Anticipation, arousal, great horror. Women reclaiming, commodifying, explotiting sexuality to alchemize a past trauma. The existential things we do to survive.

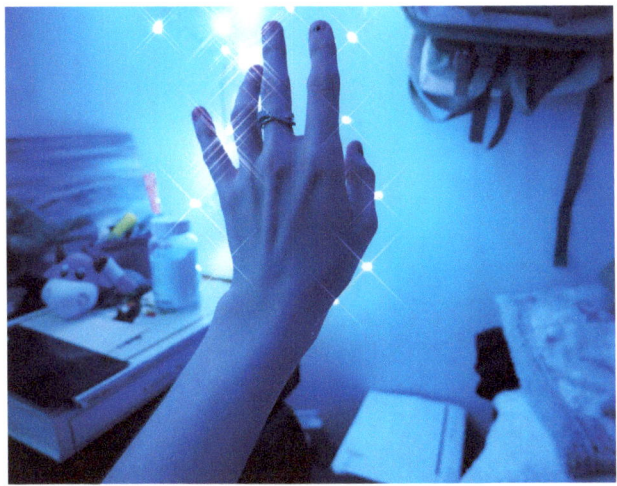

Whores are witches, fairies, angels, devils, nymphs, nymphos, scientists, healers, computer viruses, nurturers, therapists, sirens, educators, psychic nurses, and dreamers.
Do you blame the bar for creating the alcoholic, or the alcoholic for going to the bar?
In general, don't be so quick as to cast blame. Don't hate the player, hate the game.

I am not grounded in reality, I am in the space desert crashing my Tesla at the intersection of art and technology.

My life architecture is not built for capitalism, I'm just a girl.

Feeding my Pig Slop in my New Tesla
LuxuryLight · 575K views · 7 months ago

Zooted on the sauce in my Tesla like it's my job.
I made that album in my Tesla wearing lingerie.

-_-

Taking a nap in my Tesla like my life depends on it.

For a minute, just be receptive. Nobody wants to be half forgotten. Forget me, or keep me in your heart. Dream about me.

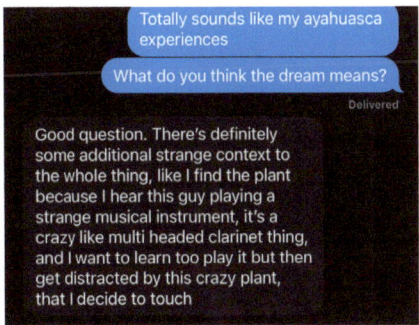

Ayahuasca was the face crack of the millennium. It was the scariest experience doing it after a seven year gap of not. The beauty and mystery and horror stops me in my tracks; a stendahl syndrome like in Chuck Palahniuk's *Haunted* (Cassandra's stories) or the deadly entertainment film in DFW's *Infinite Jest*.

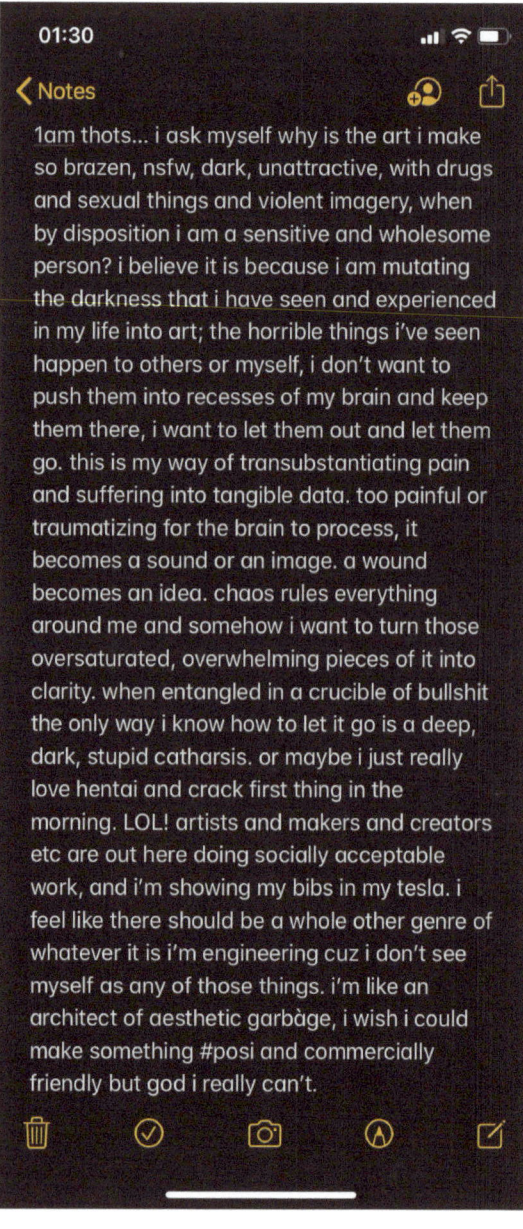

hey idiots, you can like or even love your job and still get exhausted by it and need breaks and boundaries and rights 🤯

I dream about moneybags, windfalls, high paid jobs, attaining capital. The wish is to never ever go back to the horrifying poverty I was raised in as the daughter of an immigrant single mother.

Why do I crave material things in a capitalist system that I despise? Girls like me need lots of stuff, fluff, softness, excess, safety, security, comfort. I never had these things as a kid, so as an adult I become a living princess. Fuzzy blankets and armies of stuffed seals. Kitten prints and pastel walls. A hot tub filled with stuffed seals, like my installation at Cyber Castle art show.

These seals are called Booba. It is their name, they are all Booba. I made an OF video a long time ago where I held the OG seal over my coochie and said that my favorite part of a woman's body is the pussy seal, and that this seal's name was Booba. From then on, they all were.

They are having a very important meeting in these cunty little chairs.

Dark night of the soul... and why I am a morning person.
Day time is nice... the night is long, hard and full of dreamin'.

My favorite part of my body is the guantanamo bay military prison CIA black site in my vagina.

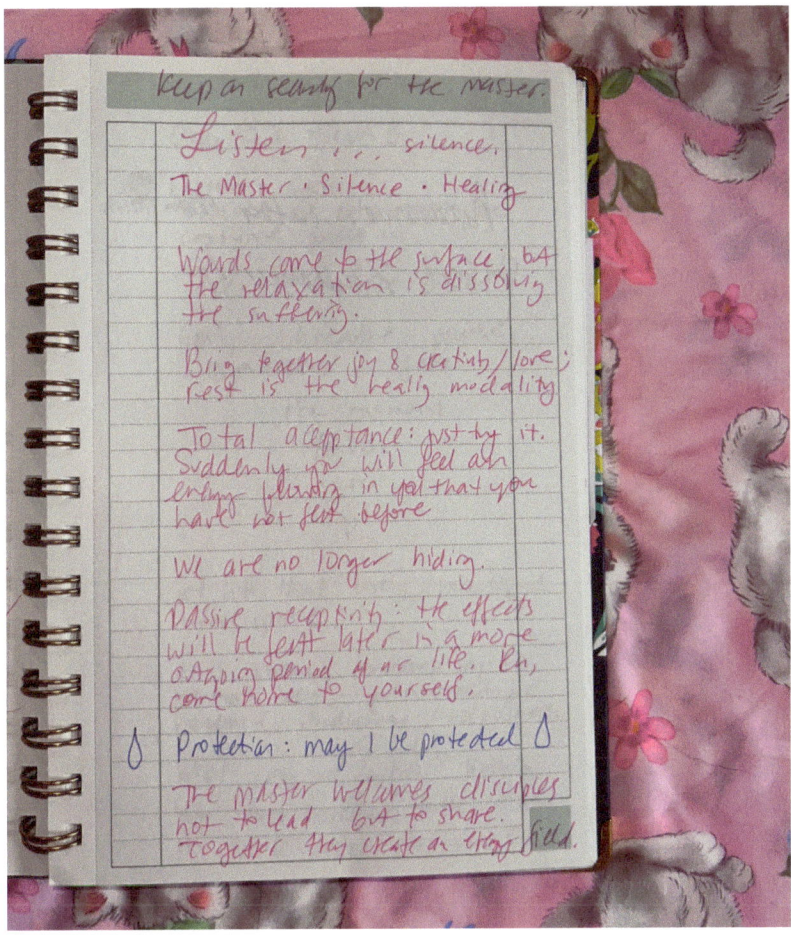

Dreaming all these dreams, I slept at night underneath my iconic Eyes Wide Shut poster. It tore during the latest remodel of my place, but once I get the McChussy Grant I will buy another one. Stanley Kubrick is a horny legend and Eyes Wide Shut is my favorite film. The entire film is a world of dreams where fantasy, alternate reality, delusion, paranoia, fidelity, transgression, eroticism, emotions, missed encounters, psychic wounds, and grandeur interweave.. Most people know this film for its "illuminati secret society orgy" scenes, but there are also deeper Lacanian interpretations in its marital narrative. This film is all about fantasy (see big L's *glissement* – a sublimation/transference where one signifier replaces another, a fantasy swapped for a bigger fantasy). In dream logic, parameters can literally replace one at any point, and anything can become anything. (In psychedelic drug experiences as well – these tools are a chemical technology into entering states of the beyond). In our tiny brains we have galaxies. That is what I believe my visionary 12/21 dream in the mediterranean restaurant with the reality-coding machine tried to imprint upon me, fusing the Lacanian with the Zen: that even in our already disposable dystopian culture, on a deeper esoteric level any element of our perceived reality can be swapped and substituted, destroyed and created, deployed and awakened, if we just close our eyes and code it into existence. A womb. A liminal space de-liminalled.

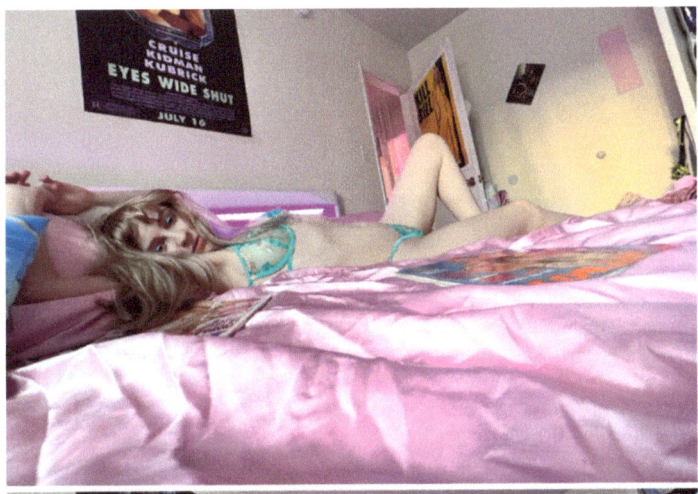

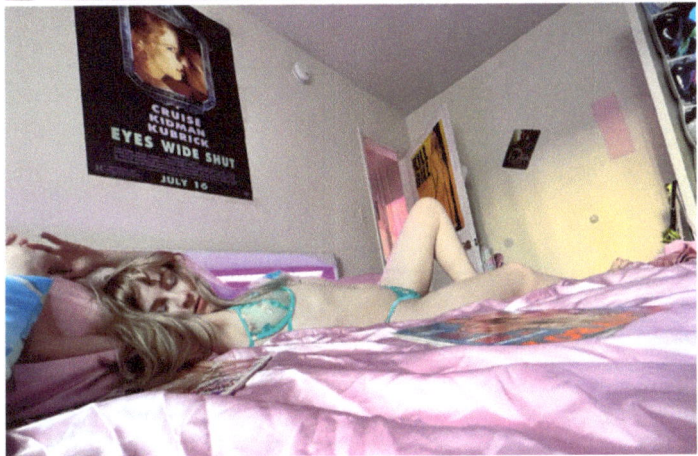

Wandering through a toy store with their daughter, after Bill confesses to her the series of fantasies he had just experienced, Alice reinforces the power of her confession (that she had once for a moment wanted to cheat). After a bumbling back and forth about their future and a consideration by Alice that "maybe" their relationship can survive this, Bill asks, "Are you … sure?" And she replies, "Am I sure? Only as sure as I am that the reality of one night, let alone that of a whole lifetime, can ever be the whole truth." Bill then responds, "And no dream is ever just a dream." -Eyes Wide Shut

These are the cat-loving scholars cyberchussing psychoanalysis and yassifying Lacanian theory in 2023:

Mon, May 1, 1:40 PM

Little booch

They like to go in the jacket

I have to run to DICKS before they close

Nastya Valentine is like if Jesse Pinkman and a wannabe 90s supermodel went to grad school and got a masters degree in sexistential economics. Her films, writing, and translation work has been seen all over the world from New York to Moscow, and her naked body may or may not have been seen all over the internet. She is the leading expert in her field - of Cyberhorny studies.

Evan Dunn is a psychoanalyst and writer. He is descended from a long line of Irish pirates and bootleggers. His works have been in trendy magazines and presented at austere conferences. His bandit ancestors used to hurl rocks across the sides of passing ships, then leap aboard and snatch any loot while the ship's crew fled below deck.

Must I cauterize my soul every morning upon waking? Are there ads in hell? Are there ads in dreams? Are we in hell if there are ads in our dreams? Or are we just in capitalism?

While Nastya embodies the aphoristic poetic-marketing speak in her voice, dissecting transactional relations and the intimacy of commerce to smash her way into a feeling, Evan's voice in contrast attempts to crawl out of the pit of marketing language, dragging feeling along with him, unlocking new circles of hell and prisms of suffering along the way. His interpretations in Part 2 of this book are invaluable to at least one psychopath.

Psychoanalysis has never left, desire never left, but we are bringing it back nonetheless. It's Jung and sexy and juicy. It's ripe as the honeys in Tuco Salamanca's telenovelas. These ripe existential mamitas are ones you cannot change the channel of. They're our deepest feelings and tragedies and projections and cognitive dissonances and catastrophizations and introjections. Our collaborations are compounded into a work in progress on the lack in our vocabulary to convey the experience of digital suffering, yearning, warring, texting, memeing, advertising, and the like. We live in an oversaturated cyber age where our minds short circuit to keep up with the pace of technology - causing mania, addiction, distraction, and dissociation. End scene.

CYBERHORNY SITE QR CODE ^

NASTYA IG^

EVAN IG^

"As things stand now, I am going to be a writer. I'm not sure that I'm going to be a good one or even a self-supporting one, but until the dark thumb of fate presses me to the dust and says 'you are nothing', I will be a writer."
— Hunter S. Thompson, <u>Gonzo</u>

"Writing is like sex. First you do it for love, then you do it for your friends, and then you do it for money."
— Virginia Woolf

NASTYA'S BANDCAMP {{cause the horny dreams need a horny soundtrack }}

Stream 'uWu' by Fembot on Spotify - my band with Celeste X

I think this one is the winner actually

Gorgeous beautiful soup and salad

Delivered

Hi yes I'd like to order the skinnylicious soup and salad combo with and side of 24oz steak lasagna sexy gorgeous abilify 10mg qd and reality testing for appetizer

20.

Two sex tapes played in a leather dungeon,
And sorry I could not watch them both
And be one pervert, long I jacked it

- Robert Frosty

Don't forget

Ur baBUSSS

Sun, May 21, 12:43 PM

Gmmmmm miss chungus

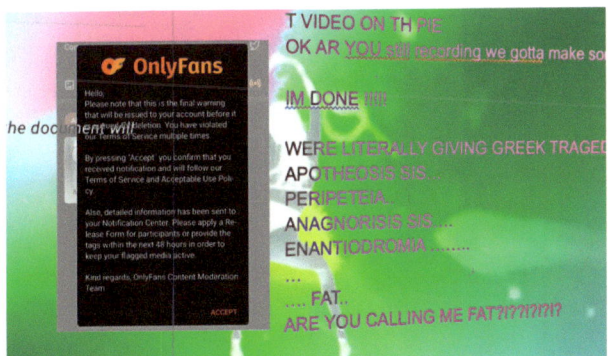

PSA: Stop being a dandy, blogger, writer, internet churl, etc.
There are already too many of us. Join the marines instead.
Wake up!
USA needs to draft less tik toks and more marine officers

Have a blessed night. 🐒 ✨

It's fucked up out here

Dreams and Nightmares by Nastya Valentine
Analysis by Evan Dunn

The Cyberhorny Dream Diaries
🐑 🐑 🐑 💕 🎀 ☁️

www.ingramcontent.com/pod-product-compliance
Lightning Source LLC
Chambersburg PA
CBHW040851120626
46547CB00006B/564